D1495159

Please return / renew by date shown.
You can renew at: **norlink.norfolk.gov.uk**
or by telephone: **0344 800 8006**
Please have your library card & PIN ready.

NORFOLK LIBRARY
AND INFORMATION SERVICE
NORFOLK ITEM

30129 077 817 758

Ho

gr

LAURENCE KING

Published in 2016 by
Laurence King Publishing Ltd
361–373 City Road
London EC1V 1LR
United Kingdom
T +44 20 7841 6900
F +44 20 7841 6910
enquiries@laurenceking.com
www.laurenceking.com

A catalogue record for this book is available
from the British Library.

ISBN: 978-1-78067-729-3

Book design: Charlie Smith Design
Cover concept: Here Design
Cover design: Charlie Smith Design
Project editor: Gaynor Sermon
Picture researcher: Peter Kent

Printed in China

Laurence King Publishing

How to have
great ideas

A guide to creative thinking

John Ingledew

Contents

Introduction:
What's the big idea?

This book is for ideas prospectors – it is a treasure map for the land of inspiration, helping you to discover ideas gold.

Each section offers a different strategy, method or line of approach to idea generation, creative thinking and problem solving. The entries also offer insights into how other people's great ideas have occurred, and practical projects help you to further explore each strategy.

What is creative thinking?

Creative thinking is the process of generating the ideas that make breakthroughs possible. These breakthroughs can lead to solutions to seemingly irresolvable problems, or can bring completely new things into existence.

Ideas are thoughts, designs, possibilities and plans that are formed through the efforts of the mind. Breakthrough ideas come from a combination of many types of mental effort, including both active and unconscious industry. This book discusses these activities and the conditions, circumstances and environments in which they can be stimulated.

Stellar ideas

Creative thinking can lead to the superstar of breakthrough ideas – an innovation. Innovative ideas lead to totally new products, or new systems, methods or services that radically improve the way that something is currently done.

The joy of ideas

Coming up with a breakthrough idea is one of the most satisfying things that we can do. Encountering a great idea can be equally enjoyable. In both situations there is an epiphany – a moment of sudden revelation. Great ideas cause a reaction, they have the power to hit you in the pit of the stomach, make the hairs on the back of your neck stand up, they can make you crack a smile or spontaneously burst into laughter or tears.

Great ideas are insistent, they excite and stay in the mind, they demand action; they can totally alter how we see things, or they can change the way that we behave.

Put your mind to work

You can use this book as a practical handbook for unleashing creativity. It will guide you through numerous methods of putting your mind to work and help you to find and develop new ideas.

Exercise your imagination

Our imaginations are what provide us with the amazing ability to kaleidoscopically rearrange thoughts, knowledge, dreams, desires and memories into new images and forms – some impossible in the real world. It is in our imaginations that we conjure up the ideas that can solve problems in exciting ways.

British writer W. Somerset Maugham remarked that 'imagination grows by exercise'. Just as athletes prepare for high jumps, hurdles or sprints by stretching and warming up, it's important to warm up and exercise the imagination so that it's nimble, mobile and speedy – ready to take flight or make great leaps.

Exercising the imagination
An art student plays the Logo Game (opposite).

Project

The Logo Game: Working in pairs, with single sheets of paper and coloured marker pens, each player draws the outlines of a familiar logo – for example, the Nike tick, Apple's bitten apple, McDonald's Golden Arches or the Olympic rings.

Exchange drawings.

Rotate the drawing you have been presented with. Turn it sideways and upside down. Look from every angle until you spot a potential way of transforming it into something completely different. Play with the shape in your mind. Treat this stage like the game in which you spot and shout out objects fleetingly made by passing clouds.

Working quickly, complete the drawing.

Now repeat with different logos.

The best idea wins. A good idea may provoke smiles or laughter – physical reactions that prove an idea has worth.

The problem is solved through the action of turning the image upside down and looking at it from different angles. However, this game also requires participants to be imaginative – you need to spot possibilities, find and make associations, and break with something that appears fixed. You also have to think quickly, be reactive to challenges and produce numerous ideas. All of these things are keys to having creative ideas, and these are further explored and developed in other sections.

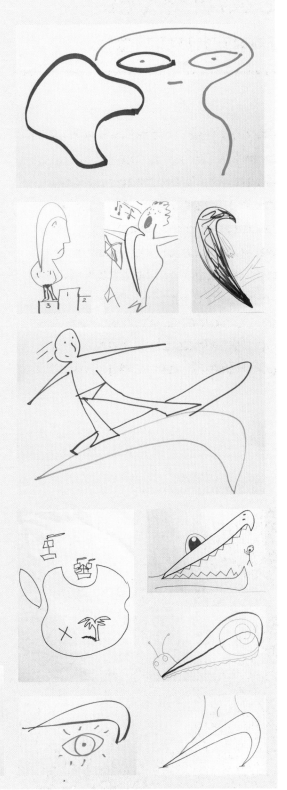

Be playful

To a child, a simple cardboard box has unlimited possibilities – as a car, plane, house, fort, post box, boat, skyscraper, spaceship, robot costume, etc. A stick or piece of wood is a *Star Wars* lightsaber, a knight's sword or a baseball bat. By being playful with any objects, words or materials you are presented with, you can reveal lots of different ideas and alternatives.

Play fighting
During playtime, found objects can take on any role. Here sticks become knights' swords.

Go out to play

Rediscover playtime – that period at school when the clock always seemed to run at a different speed. You can become lost in play. It is joyful and carefree; the ordinary rules of daily life are temporarily suspended and the form and scale of objects are overthrown and happily ignored. Designer Ron Arad describes his London studio as 'a progressive playground'. Though often seen as anarchic or chaotic, the playground is in fact the most creative place in every school. Existing configurations of walls, railings, fences and posts are constantly repurposed to invent games and found objects utilized as tools and play equipment. It is in playgrounds that young people display so many of the skills that are highly prized in creative adults – spontaneity, improvisation, ingenuity, verbal dexterity, invention, enthusiasm, collaboration and teamwork.

Some creative companies and experimental education programmes have learnt a lot from this. They have sidelined computers and instead built work environments with plenty of access to construction and modeling materials so that ideas can swiftly become objects. They set out to create a environment of shared space, and the liberated feeling of playtime in which your role as a participant is simply to mess around freely with a project and toy with ideas.

Playing with boxes
At playtime, every object offers unlimited possibilities.

Playtime 1928/29
Artist Josef Albers and his Bauhaus students, creating cardboard constructions through playful experimentation.

For this to be successful you need to be in a playful state of mind and feel that others are valued playmates rather than colleagues. (*See also* Exercise Your Imagination, page 8, and Change the Room, page 102.)

Put your game face on

The Bauhaus teacher Josef Albers believed that the hands-on gathering of experience though play with materials led to invention and was key training for all types of design work. Bearing this in mind, treat challenges as play rather than work. Put your game face on.

'The worthiest works of all often reflect an artful creativity that looks more like play than work.'

James Ogilvy, author of
Living Without a Goal

Playtime 2015
Through playing with technology and materials, today's design students discover for themselves new ways in which things can be combined and used.

Project

Using only cardboard boxes, create
prototypes of chairs you would be proud
to own. No glue and no other materials.
Chair 1 – you can only tear the card.
Chair 2 – you may use scissors.

Project

Create music with only plastic drinking cups and scissors. Play with the cups to discover as many different types of sound as you can. Play and record a plastic cup symphony.

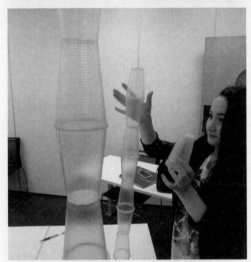

Project

Play with words. Play hide and seek – find and collect words hiding within other words.

Write your manifesto

A manifesto is a public declaration of the beliefs and objectives of an individual or a group. Numerous art movements have used manifestos to announce new and radical intentions.

Many consist of quick-fire bullet points of fighting talk, making a call to arms. The best are battle cries that inspire others to swiftly join up and follow. See those by the Surrealists, Dadaists, De Stijl and the Situationists.

Look also at mottos and mantras – concise statements of intent and conviction. The Eames studio motto was 'Create the best, for the most, for the least', and the mantra of the Modernist movement was 'Form follows function', while large-lettered banners in the Californian studios of product-development company IDEO prompt staff to 'Encourage wild ideas' and 'Build on the ideas of others'.

Don't default

Manifestos, mottos and mantras are visible reminders to stick to your guns, not to let your ideas down and not to forget your principles when starting a new challenge. They command you not to default – the desire of the mind to avoid trying something new by returning to something that is usual or standard.

Tasty stuff
An edible manifesto by design student Tom Mitchell.

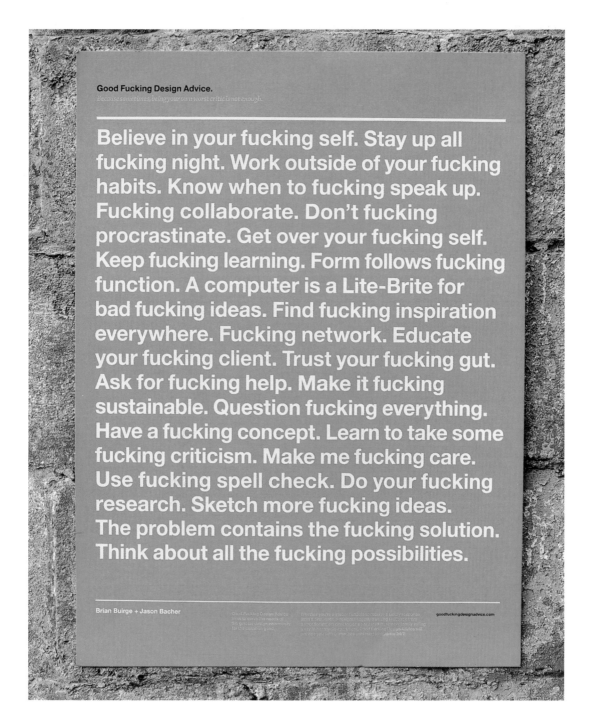

Good Fucking Design Advice
This fabulously foul-mouthed manifesto – which simultaneously inspires and insults – was created by Brian Buirge and Jason Bacher.
See www.goodfuckingdesignadvice.com

Keeping it simple
Designer Johnny Firewater's
five-word manifesto.

Creativity = Play. Don't play safe!

Project

....

Come up with a manifesto or motto
for yourself. Clarify and state your own
creative standpoint. What do you believe in?
What are you trying to achieve?

Lego manifesto (left)
Design student Laura Martin's Lego
manifesto. (See Be Playful, page 10.)

Explosive stuff (above)
One art student's call to arms.

Question, question, question

Ruthlessly interrogating a problem will extract information that leads to ideas. Use questions to challenge assumptions – things that seem to be accepted as certain or true. See the problem as a puzzle, and use questions to gather as many pieces as possible by methodically establishing as many facts as you can.

'There is only one stupid question in this world, and that is the question that does not get asked.'

Proverb

Rod Shaw, **Question, question, question ..., 2015**
See www.nonpareilpress.co.uk

Don't be afraid to ask

The barrier created by thinking 'I may make a fool of myself if I ask this' can mean that starting points and new directions for thinking remaining undiscovered. Always ask those questions that seem too obvious, or those you think you're supposed to know the answers to. When industrial designer Kenneth Grange was briefed to develop new express trains for British Rail in the 1970s, a seemingly naïve question popped into his head: 'What exactly are the buffers on a locomotive for?' Expecting to be told 'They're to stop the trains crashing into stations, stupid!', instead he learnt that they were for shunting carriages – a redundant activity from a bygone era. Liberated from the need to include them, Grange was able design the streamlined trains that went on to revolutionize rail travel in Britain.

The questioning process can be freed up in various ways – for example, by writing down all the things you're afraid to ask and swapping them with other team members so that you voice the queries of others; by establishing that everyone must ask questions in turn; or by reversing the embarrassment of seeming overly eager by saying 'Put your hand up if you don't have a question'. (*See also* Be Contrary, page 172.)

Use questions to open up a problem

American graphic designer Bob Gill uses questions as a strategy to help him solve design and advertising challenges smartly; his mantra being 'Defining a unique problem will inspire a unique solution' (*see also* Write Your Manifesto, page 16). When asked to design ads for an Italian exhibition coming to England he asked himself, 'How can I make Italy come to

England?' To create a moving card for a couple he asked, 'When a couple moves, what do they actually move?' Gill's design for a spectacular peace monument in New York was inspired by the question 'What would peace look like?' This led to the thought that, if wars ceased, the whole world would be littered with tonnes and tonnes of military scrap metal, which could be combined to form a massive sculpture mounted on a marble plinth.

Thomas Heatherwick's studio in London uses questions to develop projects, new uses for materials and new working methods. Asking questions such as 'Can you make a building using only two components?' and 'Does a window have to be flat?' has led to discoveries and outcomes impossible to predict at the time of asking. Most memorably the studio asked 'How do you let every country in the Olympic Games take part in the making and lighting of the Olympic Cauldron?' (*See also* other questioning strategies: Ask 'What Else Can I Do With This?', page 58, and Find an Analogy, page 90.)

Project

Develop questioning skills by holding a conversation entirely in questions. Can you answer every question with a question?

Keep it simple

Simplify and personalize the problem

Problems are often obscured by an overload of information. Clarify and isolate the challenge you face by spending time understanding and defining the problem. Can you simplify it down to ten words, five words or even just three? Ask yourself, 'What is the one thing I am being asked to do?' Doing this can make the quest to find a solution personal and exciting. Reduce and clarify – boil down ingredients to gain intensity and get to the essence of the challenge.

Simplify the solution

The simplest ideas are often the ones that expand the most to fill the viewer's imagination. Seek the most economical means to deliver your idea.

How simple can it be?

The Crystal Palace, built to house the Great Exhibition in London in 1851, was then the largest glass structure in the world. Remarkably, it was designed by architect Joseph Paxton to be constructed using only 48 components – each ordered by the thousand. Similarly, Barnes Wallis designed a massive airship that used only 11 different parts, while Thomas Heatherwick built a building from just two repeated components, and Thomas Edison created houses that used just one pour of concrete.

'To complicate is easy. To simplify is difficult.'
Bruno Munari, artist and designer

'Maximum meaning, minimum means.'
Designer Abram Games' manifesto (see *also* Write Your Manifesto, page 16)

'Creativity is making the complicated simple.'
Charles Mingus, jazz musician

'Good design is as little design as possible.'
Dieter Rams, designer

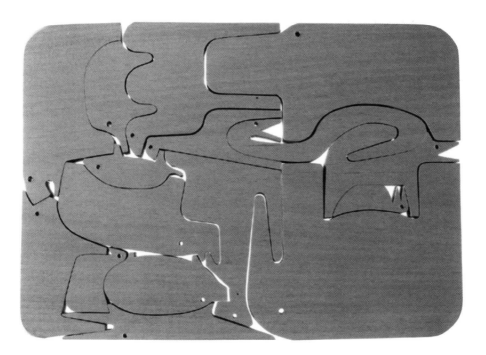

Enzo Mari, *16 Animali*, 1959
Italian designer Mari's wonderfully
simple puzzle, featuring 16 slotted-
together animals.

Project

....

Tabloid newspaper headlines seek to
simplify complex news items into as few
words as possible. The story that British
prime minister David Cameron drove off
from a pub, accidentally leaving his baby
daughter behind in her pram, was famously
encapsulated in one word by a UK tabloid:
'CAMNESIA!'

Write a headline for the following news
stories:

Star Wars fans arrive in Venice for
a convention.

An undersea cable is severed, meaning that
the internet is shut down for a day in the
United States and Europe.

Project

....

Writer Ernest Hemingway famously laid
down a challenge to write a story in six
words. Try it, or update this to a Twitter
challenge and write an entire story in just
140 characters.

Just get started

Got a challenge to solve? Want to create something new from scratch, or got half an idea you think might be worth pursuing? Just get started. Get something – anything – down on paper or on screen. It doesn't have to be coherent or structured at this stage.

Don't be precious. You can begin by simply writing down your first thoughts and then anything connected with them that comes to mind. Be broad and bold. Don't lose sight of your manifesto and fight your inner critic – that cynical voice inside your head that says 'This won't work', or even, 'Give up now!'

Learning how to get yourself started on a project is an important step towards understanding your own creative process.

'You've got to just start, that's the hardest part.'
Graham Linehan, Irish comedy writer

'Whenever I start I'm always amazed – well that wasn't so bad!'
Frank Gehry, architect

'You've often got to get it wrong before you can get it right, and then you develop it from there.'
Stan Wilson-Copp, engineer and inventor

Project

**Just get started on ....
Fill in the title of your latest project here.**

Jimmy Turrell, *The Best Way*, 2014
See www.jimmyturrell.com

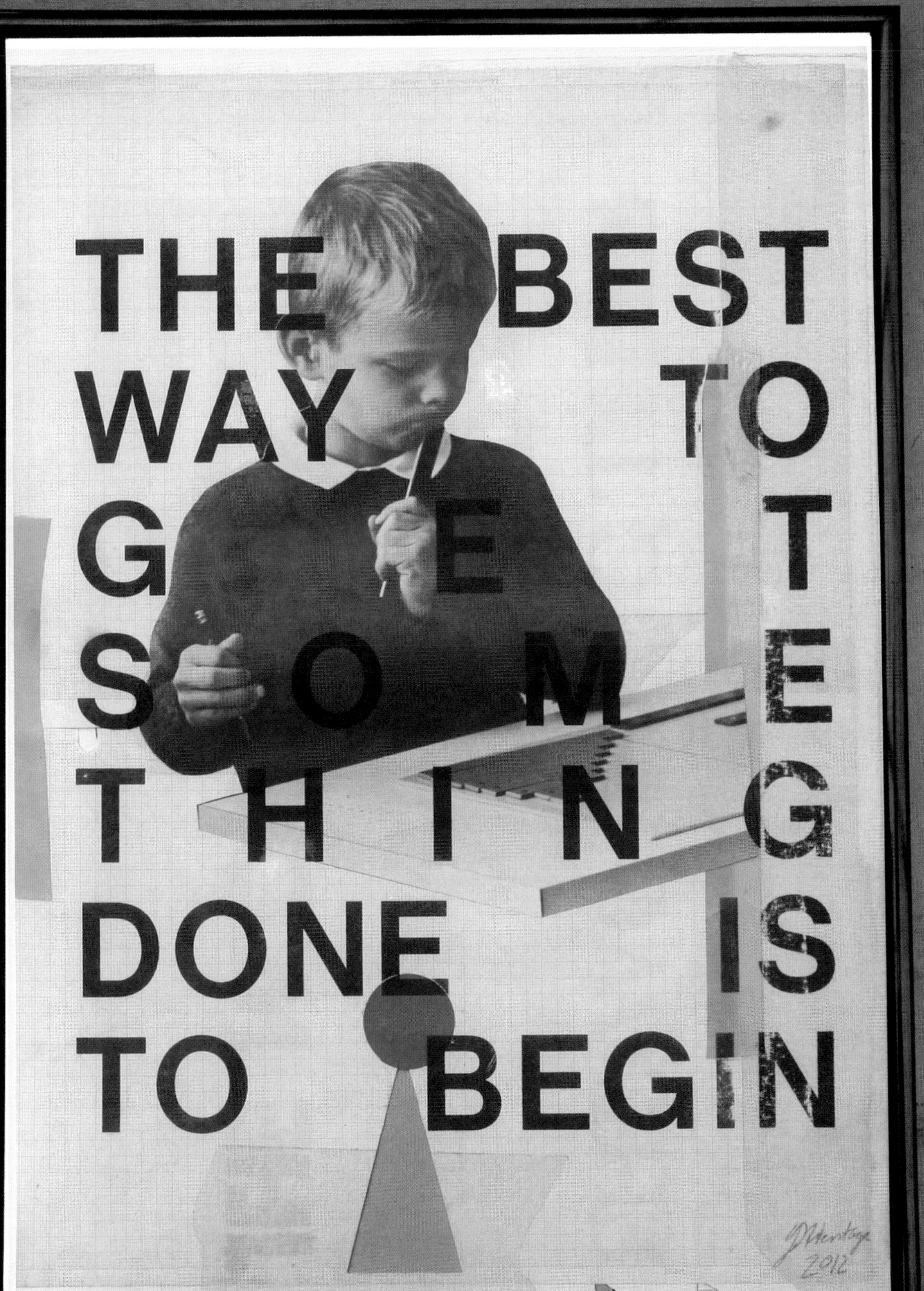
THE BEST
WAY TO
G E T
S O M E
T H I N G
DONE IS
TO BEGIN

Value first ideas

There is a great temptation to reject all first ideas, feeling they have arrived too soon, but every so often the first idea is the perfect idea.

The instant your brain is presented with a challenge, it momentarily goes into a state of confusion – it spins like slot machine reels, without logic or method. If you are lucky, you might just hit the jackpot with this fleeting frenzy, spilling out thoughts that would be inaccessible by other means.

Always consider your first idea, that impulsive response that just pops into your head. First ideas can help focus the problem and also help form subsequent ideas.

Project

....

**Collect and collate your first ideas.
Think of a title for this collection.**

Make a flying start

Never overlook the ideas that come to mind at the start. Sometimes those first-off-the-blocks flashes of inspiration are the best.

Voice your wildest concept

International motor shows display the latest lines from car manufacturers – usually featuring last year's models with just tiny modifications to styling and colour. Far more interestingly, they also show these companies' wildest and most radical ideas.

The manufacturers call these their 'concept cars'. These creations enable them to sidestep their inherent fear of the ridicule that can come from the media, their competitors or the public as a result of thinking differently. A fear of derision or humiliation means that many great ideas often go unsaid in classes, labs and the workplace; it often seems to take success, a fancy job title or high status to feel confident enough to share your thinking. Get over this fear of humiliation and always voice your wildest ideas.

Moritz Waldemeyer, LED Halo hat, 2012 (opposite)

Hats off to the German designer Moritz Waldemeyer for creating this extraordinary headgear, for a fashion show by the Irish milliner Philip Treacy. LED lights on spinning blades create a pulsing ethereal halo around the wearer's head.

Hussein Chalayan, Metamorphic dress, 2007 (above)

Hussein Chalayan is renowned for his innovative use of materials and technology. His shows feature ideas that amaze. These dresses from his 'One Hundred and Eleven' show slowly transform into different shapes and styles from fashion history. (Try asking 'What Else Can I Do With This?', page 58.)

Quirky QWERTY (opposite)
The fashion industry loves wild ideas – as seen here in Mary Katrantzou's fantastic typewriter dress.

A wild train of thought (above)
Moving Platforms is a highly innovative idea by designer Paul Priestman in which you can travel from your local stop to any destination – even in another country – without getting off a train and without stopping.
See www.priestmangoode.com

An up-in-the-clouds idea
'Aircruise' is a modern-day luxury
airship hotel, created by designers
Seymourpowell – an idea that breaks
with all established thinking about travel
and holidays. Here you travel very, very
slowly and the flight is the destination,
not the means of getting there.
See www.seymourpowell.com

What's your wildest idea?
Visuals by design students created
in response to the brief, 'What's your
wildest idea?' (See Visualize It, page 44.)

Not all industries are like the motor industry.
Fashion – both design and photography – has
always been a field that demands and applauds
the wildest and most extreme ideas.

The same can be true of architecture. The
brilliant group Archigram only ever proposed
hypothetical ideas rather than designs that
could be built – for example, the Walking City
that could roam through the landscape, and the
Plug-In City, an interchangeable framework of
standardized dwellings. The influence of this
radical thinking has been huge and can be
seen in buildings such as the Centre Pompidou,
as well as the development of the Critical
Design movement.

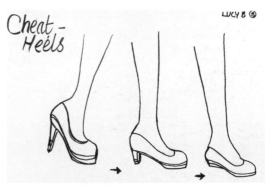

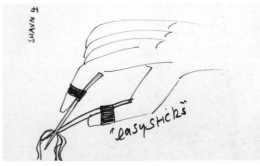

Project

Be inspired by Archigram and propose some
wild ideas for future cities.

Act like a kid

Shedding the constraints of adult life and acting like a kid again can be immensely productive when setting out to generate ideas. Children dive unstoppably into activities with an enthusiasm rarely seen in adults – totally unperturbed by what their peers may say or think.

Kids are immensely imaginative, fired by the intensely creative worlds of fairy tales, nursery rhymes, cartoons, Pixar, Disney and Nick Park movies, and books by authors such as Roald Dahl, Maurice Sendak and Dr Seuss. Dahl – like other highly creative individuals including Pablo Picasso, Thomas Heatherwick and Paul Smith – had a childlike quality himself: 'I go down to my little hut, where it's tight and dark and warm, and within minutes I can go back to being six or seven or eight again' (*see also* page 109).

Make-believe

Act like a kid and rediscover the highly creative process of playing make-believe, in which any object can be repurposed, and a dressing-up box full of old clothes has seemingly infinite potential. (*See also* Be Playful, page 10, and ask 'What Else Can I Do With This?', page 58.)

Children are unafraid to voice their wildest thoughts and questions. It was a child that exposed the fact that the Emperor was naked, when all adults were convinced he wore regal robes. Overcome the adult fear of ridicule when asking questions. Instead, always ask all

'When I was a child I wanted to be an envelope and travel the world.'

Cal, circus performer, County Down

'The photographer must look with the eyes of a child who sees the world for the first time.'

Bill Brandt, photographer

'For me, comedy is about being allowed to be a child, to make things up and to be silly, to play pretend and not be embarrassed in front of the person you are playing pretend with.'

Jennifer Saunders, comedy writer and performer

the childlike, apparently naïve questions that come to mind (*see also* Question, Question, Question, page 20, and Voice Your Wildest Concept, page 28).

Taking notice of the directness and innocence of their own children's questions has led to breakthrough ideas for many adults. Roy Lichtenstein began painting comic strip imagery after being asked 'Hey Dad, why can't you paint anything as good as cartoons?', at a stroke turning his career from failed painter to leading American artist. Similarly, English author Roger Hargreaves began writing his bestselling Mr Men books after his son asked 'What does a tickle look like?', while American scientist and inventor Edwin Land was inspired to create the innovative instant-photography Polaroid camera after his daughter asked 'Why can't I see the pictures now?'

'I guess kids are so imaginative because during their sleeping hours their minds are still filled with the excitement of bedtime stories.'

John Firewater, designer

Playing make-believe
Alice helps Tweedledum and Tweedledee prepare for pretend battle. A saucepan, coal scuttle, tray and other household objects are imaginatively combined to create the twins' armour. An illustration by John Tenniel from *Through the Looking Glass*, by Lewis Carroll.

Project

Picasso declared that 'Every child is an artist', adding, 'the problem is how to remain an artist once we grow up'. Reflecting on this, and his own training and career as an artist, Grayson Perry said 'It took me four years to be able to draw like Raphael, but it would take me a lifetime to regain anything like the joyful freedom I felt when I played with a box of Lego.' Get that box of Lego down from the loft and just dive in. Lego has been used highly imaginatively for typography, animation, fashion design, for the iPod prototype, and for music videos – famously in The White Stripes' 'Fell in Love with a Girl' promo, which was directed by Michel Gondry.

Take notice

Get the habit of curiosity, and then you will find ideas will catch your eye. Always be on the lookout for interesting things.

'Creative people are expert noticers' observed scientist Professor Guy Claxton. They have highly developed abilities in visual foraging – spotting, gathering and utilizing things that most others overlook. Having an active, rather than idle, curiosity about the world around you reveals ideas. Be nosey, be eyesy.

'To be creative, you have to be curious.'

Philippe Starck, designer

'Curiosity is the lust of the mind.'

Thomas Hobbes, philosopher

Visual treasure (this page)
Embracing chairs, rushing men and a puzzling bike spotted in the street.

Horse play (opposite)
Look out for moments in which chance new relationships are formed between things. Photographer Peter Dench spotted this at the races.

Begin by looking for the visual treasure that your surroundings throw up. When chance new relationships are formed between things, juxtapositions that would be impossible to invent often occur. Look for the things that frustrate, and things that don't working (*see also* Fix Your Frustrations, page 96). Look for ways in which the urban and rural environment is used in ways it was not designed for – these are often highly ingenious (*see also* Find Your Ingenious Inner Genius, page 66).

To see things afresh, try taking a different route to somewhere you often go, or travel by a different means; break your usual pattern, go slower, go faster – you will see things differently. Collect and record what you discover with a cameraphone, camera or a notebook.

'You just need to step outside and pay attention to what is so commonplace, so everyday, so mundane that everyone else misses it.'

Gavin Pretor-Pinney, author and founder of the Cloud Appreciation Society

Noticing opportunity (opposite, top)
Observation can reveal opportunity – 'Looks like cyclists can't find waterproof saddles! Hey, I could invent one.'

Noticing need (opposite, below)
Observation can reveal need – there needs to be a rubbish bin here.

Noticing ingenuity (below)
Look out for instances of familiar things being used in new ways – London railings lend themselves to many unexpected functions and a Shanghai bicycle repair man adopts a phone box as his office on a chilly day (*see also* page 150).

Project

Spot and collect the faces, animals, letterforms and numbers that are accidentally created by wear, repair, time, decay, spillage, breakage, update, replacement, light, shadow, rain or snow. Some of these things only reveal themselves when you look at them sideways, upside down or in reverse.

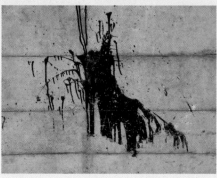

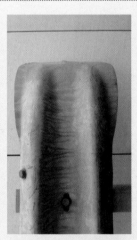

Visualize it

The simple act of drawing an idea helps develop it: initial ideas can be indistinct and fragile, and visualizing helps these quarter- or half-formed ideas become fully formed. The process of translating thoughts in your head via your hand into a drawing helps them evolve and solidify. You don't have to be 'good at art', just scribble, doodle or scrawl. In advertising, ideas committed to paper are known as scamps or thumbnails; in film-making they are called storyboards.

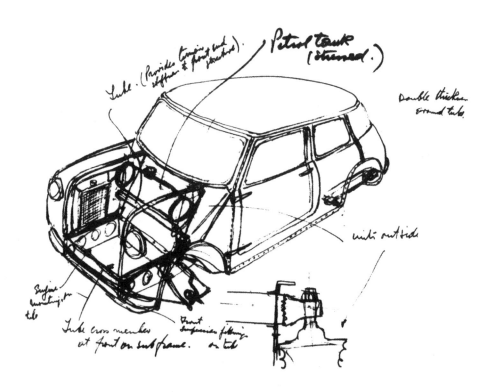

We seem to have an inner drive to visualize at the moments when ideas suddenly crystallize in the mind. These fleeting seconds of clarity should be seized and acted upon. There is a long tradition of 'back of the envelope/napkin' ideas – where the nearest material to hand has been hastily grabbed to commit ideas to paper.

Joseph Paxton hurriedly visualized the revolutionary design of the Crystal Palace building on the back of a restaurant carriage napkin while waiting at a station between trains, and Alec Issigonis jotted the details for the innovative engineering of the Mini car on the back of envelopes. While on a beach in Wales, the engineer Maurice Wilks used the only material to hand to get down his initial ideas for the Land Rover vehicle – drawing his thoughts in the wet sand. Visualizing helps share ideas with others too, including partners, collaborators and clients. Terry Gilliam remarked that whilst directing his films, 'drawing is often the easiest way to communicate with people – it gives other people ideas, whether it's costumes, sets or cameramen'.

'Doodling is the brooding of the mind.'

Saul Steinberg, artist

'Visualization helps you to begin to make new connections between things.'

**Ross Cooper,
multidisciplinary designer**

'When I try to imagine a film, lots of new ideas occur by simply trying to draw it.'

Terry Gilliam, animator and film director

Mini drawings (opposite)
Alec Issigonis's visuals for the revolutionary Mini. Amazingly, Issigonis originated almost the entire design and specification of the cars on the backs of envelopes and, apparently, even a tablecloth. (*See also* Change What Appears to be Fixed, page 93.)

Eye-deas (above)
Here some Chinese art students display their ideas in visual form during a group project to create a massive drawing that can be best seen from passing aircraft. The idea that was eventually chosen was a drawing of an eye.

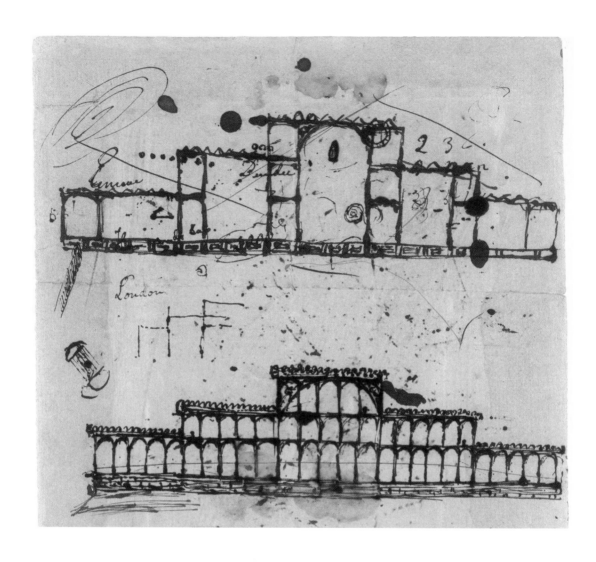

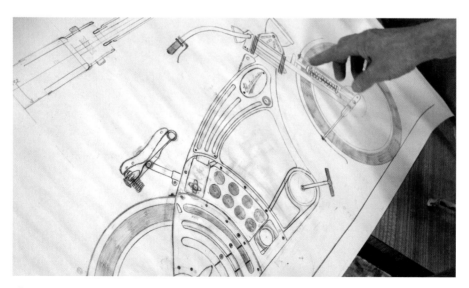

Get it down so you don't let it down

The visualization of ideas helps you see the qualities and merits of various different options, and also helps with the process of elimination. It plays a vital part in clarifying, simplifying and getting to the essence of your thoughts, ensuring you don't let a really good idea down through over-elaboration when it comes to its execution. Nick Pride, a designer and design teacher offers this advice: 'If you're in a period of stimulating thought and things are occurring to you with rapidity it's necessary to get them out. If you don't you're going to get confused. Drawing out everything that's in your mind gets rid of the ideas that you've used before that clutter your brain. Get these down, know that they're out of your mind, then you can turn the page and get on to the new.'

Sharing ideas
These European and Chinese design students are sharing their ideas in a global language – drawing.

Crystallizing ideas (opposite, top)
Joseph Paxton's visual for the Crystal Palace, drawn on the back of a napkin.

Electric ideas (opposite, bottom)
Visuals for the head-turning 'Electric Cruise' bike, designed by Jack Wimperis. See jackwimperis.com

'Visualizing is simply recording your thinking. Its value is that when taking something half-formed in the brain into a visual form on paper – where it physically exists – you are forced to make a set of decisions that moves the process on and contributes to the idea evolving.'

Nick Pride, designer and design teacher

Project

Practise visualizing by drawing things that are unseeable in the real world.

What does your creative brain look like?

What does the brain of a mathematician look like?

What does the brain of a musician look like?

Visualize different forms of music – jazz, rumba, salsa, rap, rave and classical.

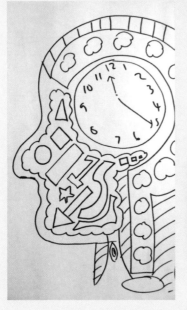

Get help

Find some collaborators. Working with others helps nurture and develop ideas. With the right people you can push yourself and your ideas much further. As the comedian John Cleese said, 'You get to a place in collaboration that you can never get to yourself'.

Double acts – double the creativity

Numerous creative fields boast highly successful partnerships: for example, in comedy, double acts Laurel and Hardy, Dawn French and Jennifer Saunders, Trey Parker and Matt Stone, and Ricky Gervais and Stephen Merchant; in music, Rogers and Hammerstein, Lennon and McCartney, Goffin and King, Leiber and Stoller, and Morrissey and Marr; in science, Crick and Watson; in aviation, Orville and Wilbur Wright; in photography Mert and Marcus, and Pierre et Gilles; in art, Gilbert and George, and Nobel and Webster; and in fashion, Dolce and Gabbana. In partnerships you can bat ideas back and forth, changing the aim, putting a spin on each other's successive play. You both shine more brightly by acting as the foil for each other.

Good partners are trusted and encouraging friends – unafraid of being judged, being knocked back or feeling stupid when suggesting thoughts to each other. Successful pairings develop a chemistry, rapport, understanding and a warm sense of competition.

Different strategies and methods develop within partnerships. The Wright brothers, for example, would swap arguments to resolve issues. The physicist Francis Crick – whose partnership with biologist James Watson led to the discovery of the DNA molecule against fierce competition – said: 'We pooled the way we looked at things. We didn't leave it that Jim did the biology and I did the physics. We both did it together, and switched roles and criticized each other, and this gave us a great advantage over the other people who were trying to solve it.'

Different generations of artists have formed themselves into such mutually supportive packs, coming together under the banner of different -isms and -ists, including the Surrealists, Dadaists, Futurists, Cubists and Impressionists. (*See also* Write Your Manifesto, page 16.)

Groups of collaborators bring many different skills and perspectives together, and a mix of like-minded and un-like-minded individuals, but to be successful there must be gang rules, mutual respect and loyalty. Hugely successful creative gangs include the writers of *The Simpsons, Saturday Night Live* and the Monty Python team, who wrote in partnerships or individually before uniting to present their ideas, and choosing democratically the work that would be included in their shows.

Get a consigliere

A knowledgeable, well-informed confidant can act as a sounding board for idea development. Consiglieres and mentors usually fulfil this role by offering experience and wisdom. In our digital age, however, the fact that younger people have a far greater understanding of developing technologies, their workings and possibilities has led to younger mentors being sought for the first time.

Gang mentality – teaming with ideas

Working with a big bunch of collaborators can be as fruitful as partnerships. You can feel yourself fiercely protected within the security of a gang that offers togetherness and camaraderie – a self-contained band of brothers or sisters united against all others.

Project

Try working to solve some of this book's challenges with a partner and in teams. Work with like-minded and un-like-minded people, and with those from other disciplines.

Know who's the daddy

Discover the fathers and godfathers of ideas and mothers of invention. Be an ideas genealogist – explore the family tree of creativity and trace the lineage of the ideas that stir you. Find the daddies, the black sheep and the bastard cousins. Learn who are the originators, the idea pioneers and trail-blazers – and those who are the tribute acts.

Follow the pioneer trail and get insights into their working methods and inspirations. Know the motherships – the organizations and establishments that nurtured those individuals that have spread key ideas globally. For example, Bauhaus, whose members disseminated Modernism and innovative teaching methods throughout the world.

The family tree of artistic movements and leading artists
Sarah Fanelli was commissioned by the Tate in London to illustrate the lineage of modern art. The result can be seen in a massive mural in the Tate Modern.

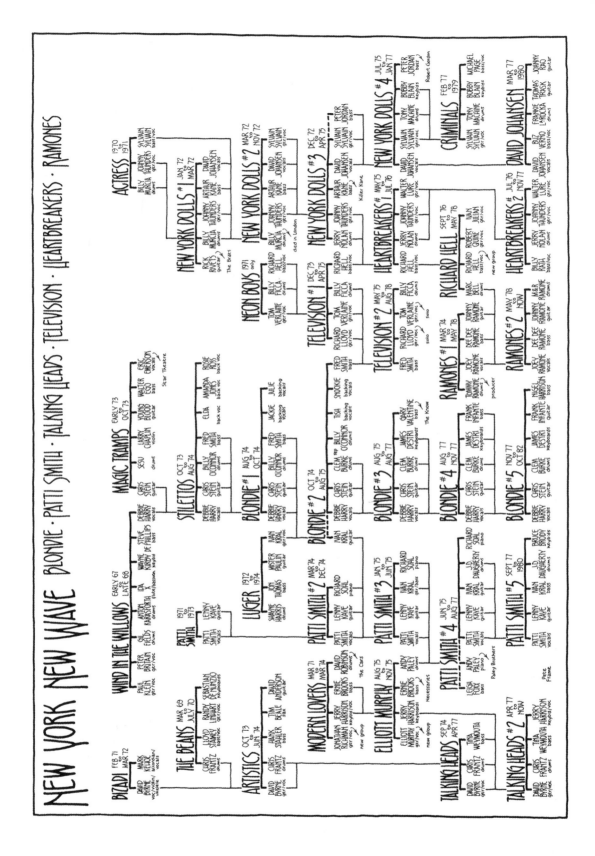

NEW YORK NEW WAVE

BLONDIE · PATTI SMITH · TALKING HEADS · TELEVISION · HEARTBREAKERS · RAMONES

Some of the ideas family

The father of modern art: Paul Cézanne

The father of Modernist architecture:
Le Corbusier

The father of modern advertising:
David Ogilvy

The father of modern chemistry:
Robert Boyle

The godfather of soul: James Brown

The father of modern physics:
Ernest Rutherford

The godmother of punk: Patti Smith

A mother of invention:
Frank Vincent Zappa

The grandmother of performance art:
Marina Abramovic

The godfather of absurdity: Isidore-Lucien
Ducasse, aka the Comte de Lautréamont

The godfather of ska: Laurel Aitken

The godfathers of acting: Marlon Brando,
Robert De Niro and Al Pacino

The modfather: Paul Weller

The father of African literature:
Chinua Achebe

The godfather of Pop art: Kurt Schwitters

The father of Pop art: Richard Hamilton

The godfather of sustainable design:
Victor Papanek

The godmother, and sister, of rock & roll:
Sister Rosetta Tharpe

The grandfather of car manufacture:
Henry Ford

The godfather of house music:
Frankie Knuckles

The mother of modern British theatre:
Joan Littlewood

The father of rock n roll: Sam Phillips

The mother of invention: Beulah Louise
Henry, awarded more than 100 patents

The father and son of engineering:
Marc Isambard Brunel and Isambard
Kingdom Brunel

The father of the blues: W. C. Handy

The father of the Delta blues: Charley
Patton

The grandfather of modern magazine
design: Alexey Brodovitch

Project

....

**Draw up a family tree interlinking
successive generations of one of the
following disciplines – advertising, stand-
up comedy, magic, street photography,
fashion photography, poetry, architecture,
taxidermy, engineering or games design.**

**The family tree of the New York
New Wave**
Over the last 30 years, journalist Pete
Frame has produced a forest of family
trees detailing every branch of popular
music. See www.familyofrock.net

What would Terry do?

The word inspiration comes from the Latin *inspirare*, meaning 'to breathe into'. Inspiration breathes life into your ideas. Find human inspiration by exploring the family tree of ideas. (*See also* Know Who's the Daddy, page 51.) Select an individual as your ideas hero or heroine – someone who hands you down ways of thinking and doing.

The inventor James Dyson cites Thomas Edison as his ideas hero, having learnt from him to make just one change to each successive prototype – a process known as iteration – so as to be certain of which elements of a design

work and which do not (*see also* Fail Towards Success, page 88).

As well as gaining major insights and learning new creative processes from your hero, you can also try their approach to problem-solving when first encountering a challenge. This can immediately start ideas flowing.

A group of the author's students christened this method of kick-starting ideas 'What would Terry do?', after their chosen ideas hero, the wild, highly controversial, maverick American photographer Terry Richardson – notorious for his contempt for traditional methods, equipment and protocol.

After channelling Terry, they would follow up by asking what Tim Walker would do? Or Dianne Arbus? Or Damien Hirst? Putting themselves in these different mindsets never failed to spark ideas speedily.

Stepping into someone else's shoes (opposite)
The owners of each of these items of footwear would approach the same challenge in very different ways. Imagine seeing the world as someone else does.

Seeing the world through Terry's eyes (below)
What on earth would Terry do with a brick? (See some possible answers on pages 60–63.)

Project

When presented with a problem think: What would Napoleon do? What would Alex Ferguson do? What would Wonder Woman do? What would Chen Man do? What would *Iron Man*'s Tony Stark do? What would your best friend do? What would Alexander the Great do?

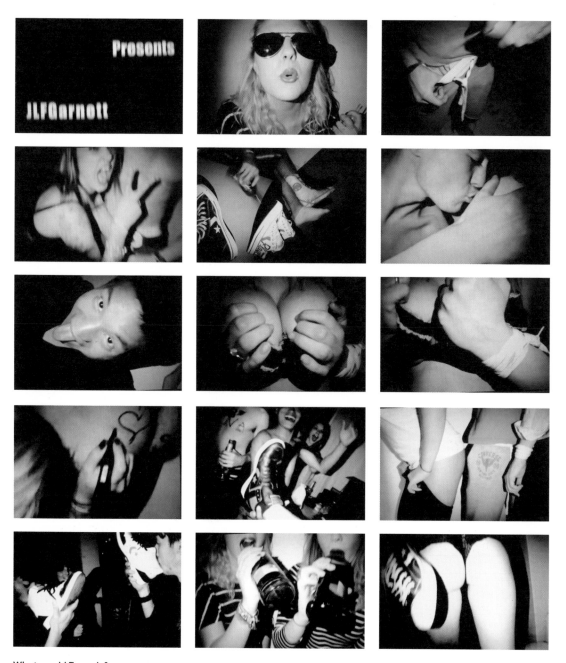

What would Terry do?
After being challenged to channel
Terry Richardson, photography student
Jonathan Garnett created this full-on
prize-winning ad for Converse clothing.
See www.jlfgarnett.com

Ask 'What else can I do with this?'

In a scene in *Alice's Adventures in Wonderland*, Alice tries to play croquet using a flamingo for a mallet, and a hedgehog for the ball, thereby revealing previously unimagined uses for both creatures.

We see most things – objects, buildings, spaces, materials, technology and systems – through the lens of habit and familiarity. We take them for granted, overlooking numerous other possibilities. Combat the mind's tendency to assume that something can only function in a familiar way. Asking yourself 'What else can I do with this?' will lead to new discoveries and ideas.

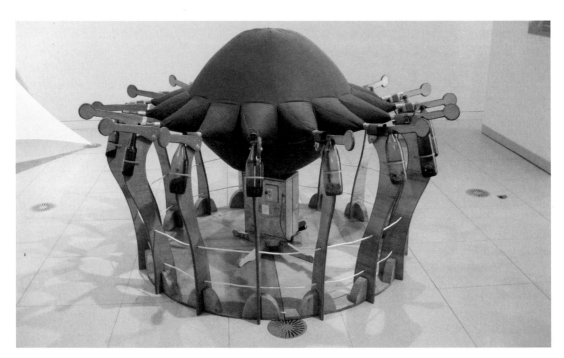

'What else can I do with old glass bottles?' (above)
Sculptor Dan Knight finds a wonderful answer in this brilliant sound sculpture. Music can by played by pressing down on the handles, causing air to blow across the neck of the variously sized bottles. See and hear his work on YouTube.

Nailed it (opposite)
Hussein Chalayan finds an unforeseen use for false nails. (See Voice Your Wildest Concept, page 28.)

'What can I do with a brick?'
Fully examining the properties of familiar objects can reveal many new possibilities – here the shape, structure, texture, volume, weight, impermeability, non-flammability and cultural history of a brick have been explored to find uses other than house building.

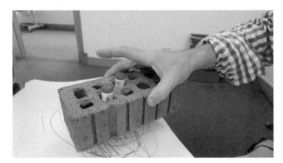

'What else can I do with a brick?'

You can print, prop, play games, transport things, create typography, measure, grate, crack nuts, make music and art, toast racks and window displays. Its limitless potential makes a brick the perfect present.

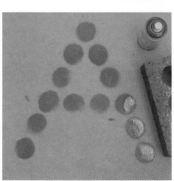

Great ideas that transform function include the Droog 'Bottoms Up' doorbell, and the use of concrete mixers as washing machines by the British Army in Afghanistan.

Forget the common uses of an object and examine instead all of its properties – strengths, weaknesses, weight, texture, smell, colour, sound, shape, volume, solidity, portability, fragility, flammability, luminosity, buoyancy, etc. What would happen if it was thrown, dropped, submerged, hit?

Ask yourself what unique properties this exploration has revealed. What could you interlink? What could you do with two or many that you cannot do with one? What else does it look like? Be playful – like Alice, and new ideas will reveal themselves.

Always ask yourself what else you could do with any new technology.

**'What else can you do with an iPad?'
(above)**
Multidisciplinary designer Jack Schulze
found this excellent new function for an
iPad, using photographic and animation
techniques to draw moving three-
dimensional typography.

**'What else can you do with a wine
glass?' (opposite)**
Peter van der Jagt of Dutch design
company Droog created the
'Bottoms Up' doorbell. Utilizing the
sound-making properties of fine crystal
glass, it announces guests with a musical
toast. This piece is held in the collections
of many design museums around the
world. See www.droog.com

Projects

....

Turn rubbish into gold – take all the junk
mail that comes through your letterbox
and turn it into something of great value.

What else can you do with a newspaper?
A corkscrew? An umbrella? A take-away
coffee lid? That thing that comes inside
pizza delivery boxes that stops the pizza
touching the inside of the lid? What else
can you do with technology – scanners,
3D printers, old computers; or imaging
technology, such as brain scanners, CT
scanners, ultrasound and thermal cameras.

Further viewing

See multiple examples of creative
refunctioning in Terry Gilliam's wonderful
short film *The Crimson Permanent Assurance*.

Find your ingenius inner genius

In *Julie and the Prince*, a play by Louis Robinson, the young king's son frets gloomily about the vast expense he will incur in building a chain of watchtowers, needed to protect the coastline of Nova Scotia and its inhabitants from enemy invasion.

Julie provides the perfect solution: 'Borrow the money from the bank. First use the loan to buy a forest. Then you commission the watchtowers. The contractors you hire will require timber, which your forest will supply. Everyone will be happy. Nova Scotia will have its defences, the people will have work and you will have the money to repay the bank, with some left over.' 'Ingenious!' shouts the prince.

Ingenuity is the ability to overcome problems by devising solutions that use and combine resources in ways few would expect.

Making a tram run up a steep hill requires a hugely powerful and expensive engine – but if you use another tram to go down simultaneously and link both with a cable to counterbalance the up-load, then you only need a very small motor on each. In addition, this solution doubles the journeys available, and halves the waiting time between trams. That's ingenious.

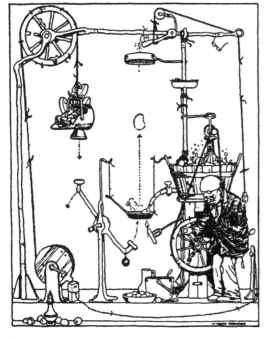

William Heath Robinson, *Pancake Making Machine*
W. Heath Robinson's wonderful drawings of inventions saw his name enter the dictionary as a synonym for absurdly ingenious devices. Note that a brick is used as a starting device. (Ask 'What Else Can I Do With This?', page 58, and see Embrace Absurdity, page 136.)

GLAZING WAGGON.

Palatial ingenuity

Many of the construction methods used by Joseph Paxton to build the Crystal Palace (see Visualize It, page 44) were highly ingenious. One example was the guttering, designed both to get rid of rainwater speedily, and to provide the tracks for small wagons to travel along to install the glass roof, thereby removing the need for massive amounts of scaffolding.

That's ingenious

Ingenuity can surprise and delight.
Here, plastic bags full of water repel
flies at a beachside restaurant on Gozo
island, old cannons keep cars out in
Havana, a wheelbarrow provides seating,
and a wheelie bin and a discarded table
leg become the equipment for a game
of cricket.

That's genius
Ingenious ways to keep your tea warm and get a suntan without getting your towel sandy.

Building ingenuity
An old work glove placed by builders over the end of a scaffolding pole prevents it from damaging woodwork.

Playful ingenuity
Books provide the bats and net for a game of ping-pong.

Blooming ingenious
Gardeners display ingenuity in finding ways to protect their plants from snails, slugs and birds using common objects.

Ingenuity is a special branch of creativity; its unexpected use of resources can instantly surprise and delight, as seen by the prince's reaction in the story. Examples of ingenuity are frequently described as 'elegant', 'neat', 'astonishing' – even 'genius!'

Creating an ingenious solution results in a huge sense of achievement. It is the result of using your inner genius to conjure success in a situation where a more complicated response might fail.

Think your way out of tricky situations. Fiercely examine the possibilities of every option, material and object available. Ask 'What else can I do with this?' (page 58). Shuffle the opportunities by looking at all the consequences and benefits that occur from interlinking what you have found in different combinations. Ingenious solutions will spring to mind.

Project

....

Create a system that transports a marble or ball-bearing across a room in the slowest way possible. Use only the things available in your kitchen – knives, forks, saucepans, plates, bowls, spaghetti, tin cans, etc.

Look at the drawings by the masters of ingenious inventions, William Heath Robinson and Rube Goldberg, and the brilliant video inspired by them, made by James Frost and Syyn Labs for the band OK Go. *See also* **the Peter Fischli and David Weiss film** *Der Lauf der Dinge* **(***The Way Things* **Go), and the UK Honda 'Cog' ad, directed by Antoine Bardou-Jacquet for agency Wieden+Kennedy.**

Shining ingenuity
Designer Jack Wimperis made this wooden iPhone mount to film the reflections made in his motorbike's chrome headlamp. You get an amazing fish-eye lens view of trees, sky and clouds as he speeds through the countryside. See jackwimperis.com

Make 'em laugh

Learning to write and tell jokes can be a shortcut to learning to think creatively. Wit has been described as 'cerebral acrobatics', and like much creativity it needs mental agility - flips, leaps and pirouettes – in order to succeed.

Publicis Frankfurt, Rowenta vacuum cleaner advert
A laugh-out-loud idea.

A joke is an idea shared with an audience. As it only takes seconds to tell, you must have loads of jokes to create a routine, which in turn is great ideas-generation practice. To write jokes you have to learn to successfully connect different things from different places – a process often described as 'joining the dots'. Joining, or connecting, the dots is also key to creative thinking, so joke writing is a great way to develop this skill. What is also useful is the fact that you instantly know whether an idea is successful or not: the response to a joke is immediate – laugher or silence.

Finding and joining the dots

Finding jokes necessitates seeking and forming unexpected connections between words, phrases or objects. Most great jokes have a kind of skewed symmetry in which two or more elements – often very disparate ones – are brought together through verbal trickery and magically snap together.

Learn to write puns

Opposite is a slogan that was created for the Roadkill Restaurant. Learning to write puns is a great place to start joke writing. Puns are a simple form of joke that exploit two different meanings of the same word or phrase. Shop owners in particular love punning names for their businesses. For example, Italian restaurants called the Leaning Tower of Pizza and Spaghetti Junction; a florist called Back to the Fuchsia; a denim store called Jeanius; and a wine merchant called Planet of the Grapes. The author's own favourite retail puns are an actor's café called First Choice for the Roll, and a wine business supplying weddings that has called itself Catching the Bouquet.

Begin by trying to write punning names for a new chain of opticians. First compile all the words you can think of associated with eyewear. Then broaden your search. Find synonyms for

'Outside of a dog, a book is a man's best friend. Inside a dog it's too dark to read.'

Groucho Marx, comedy genius (See also Embrace Absurdity, page 136.)

'From your grille to ours'

Ad for the Roadkill Restaurant

Visual jokes
In each picture two elements are brought together in unexpected ways.

the words you have found – words that have the same or similar meaning. Think of popular books, songs, TV programmes and movies that include any of the words you have found. Think of slang words, clichés, phrases, rhymes and expressions associated with eyes, spectacles and spectacle wearers.

These things are your dots. Now you have to find connections amongst them. Establish which words have more than one meaning, or mean something else if spelt differently. Join the dots by spotting overlaps, intersections and coincidences. This is where you have to make the leaps and pirouettes to build on what you have found.

Some possibilities: Spectacular; I can see clearly now; Eye, Eye, Captain; For Eyes; For Your Eyes Only; Specs in the City; Len's Lenses; Optical Nerve; Eyes Right; Eye-deal; V eye P; Eye'll be seeing you; A touch of glass; Eye Browse; Op-tick; Visual-Eyes; Op-tickle: The Sight Site; Eye to Eye Contacts; Buy Focals; Shady Deals; To see or not to see; Eye Site; I wear; Glamour Eyes; Special Eyes; and Perfect Pupils.

'The creative process is … most clearly revealed in humour and wit.'

Arthur Koester, author of *The Act of Creation*

'I used to work in a shoe-recycling shop. It was sole-destroying.'

Alex Horne, stand-up comedian

Project

1. Write punning names for:
   A store that sells trainers
   A nail bar
   A café for photographers

2. Photograph a series of visual jokes.

Reposition

The action of altering how something is viewed can reveal new possibilities and ideas. This can be achieved by seeking every possible viewpoint and by shifting context – by taking things from their usual home and placing them somewhere completely different.

**Vivienne Westwood and Jamie Reid,
Sex Pistols T-shirt (Previous)**
Westwood and Reid's act of turning
T-shirts inside out before printing made
the machine-stitched seams and labels
a feature of their now legendary designs.

Robin Rhode, *He Got Game*, 2000
A slam-dunk idea from South African
artist Rhode – photographing from a
bird's eye view to create the illusion of
a spectacular basketball score.

Fred Astaire in *Royal Wedding*, 1951
In a scene from this film, the lovestruck
lead, played by Fred Astaire, is suddenly
able to dance upside down on the ceiling.
It is simply brilliant – as an idea, in its
execution, and for Astaire's apparently
gravity-defying performance.

Boxes of wire scrubbing pads and cans of soup are familiar items in a supermarket; there are unmade beds in every teenager's bedroom; and dead cows and sheep can be found in the back of every butcher's shop, but put them in an art gallery and they are big news. Nearly 100 years ago, Marcel Duchamp was the first artist to realize that such repositioning could have impact when his submission to an art exhibition of a porcelain urinal laid flat on its back caused an enormous scandal.

Shifting viewpoint and placing the familiar in unfamiliar surroundings triggers new thoughts as shapes and forms are seen afresh and have to be reconsidered. Functions taken for granted are overturned and totally new meanings can become apparent.

Daniel Eatock, felt pen drawings, 2011
Eatock creates great coloured drawings by placing paper on top of upturned marker pens. The pens' function has totally changed in this shift, as they now make their own mark. Eatock creates work for museums, galleries, television, cinema, design, advertising, branding and education. See eatock.com

Project

....

Make the unremarkable remarkable – go to a builder's merchant and find an inexpensive object that, through repositioning in the home, finds a surprising new purpose.

Hoard

Everyone collects music – everyone has their own unique hoard; no one's top 50 is the same. We gather particular songs because they have strong meaning for us, saving them because they transport us to special places of happiness, sadness or even into states of elation. We collect them – rejecting most others – because they are the most personally potent.

Spot and collect ideas, objects, stories, jokes, photos, adverts, words, typography, colours and patterns of speech in a similar way, together with examples of innovative thinking, ingenuity and improvisation. Choose those things that stand out for you personally – things that speak to you in the same way that your favourite songs do.

This stockpile will be revealing. Collecting clarifies understanding, and it develops both skills and knowledge. It highlights the methods that communicate to you and excite you the most, offering models to be further investigated, learned from, applied or adapted. Look for patterns, interrelationships, gaps and oddities in your hoard. Use these as starting points to inspire your own ideas and creativity. Your collections are pieces of a jigsaw that, once assembled, can help you develop your own preferred ways of working (see Understand Your Process, page 176).

....

'My thoughts on creativity are partly formed through my collection of scrapbooks in which I have squirrelled away examples of innovative thinking that moved me in some way.'

**Marc Lewis,
advertising teacher**

....

'I would write down lots of things, things people said at work that were funny, conversations I heard. I have got books of them.'

Peter Kay, comedian

....

Project

....

Become attuned to things that stand out for you from the everyday and the mundane. Collect the things that speak to you above the hubbub of daily noise. Look out in particular for those that shout.

A hoard of treasure
Posters, signage, tickets and objects amassed and treasured by designer and teacher Nick Pride.

Find a link

Ideas in visual communication are often incredibly simple in form. Some of the best ideas in graphic design, advertising and illustration are so simple that they employ just two elements. It is the interaction between these that creates a reverberation in the minds of viewers, and reveals the idea.

To succeed in creating such ideas it is necessary to seek, find and unite two pertinent pieces that, when combined, express the message you wish to communicate. Gather as many relevant images as you can in front of you. Play with them. Seek connections of shape, form or language. Explore every possibility of connection until a successful link appears.

McDonald's get the builders in
Ad agency DDB Copenhagen find perfect visual links between the two key elements of this story – builders and McDonald's. The poster read 'McDonald's in Birkerød re-opens in 3 weeks'.

Recycling the Olympic rings (opposite)
Oscar-winning film-maker and graphic designer Arnold Schwartzman created this poster, brilliantly interlinking the Olympic logo with sport. (See the Logo Game, page 9.)

ABSOLUT ATHENS.

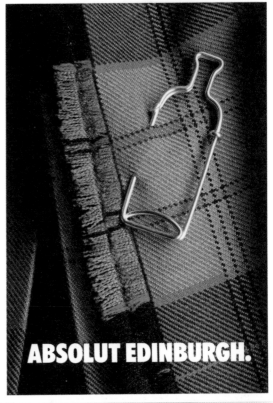

ABSOLUT EDINBURGH.

ABSOLUT ROME.

ABSOLUT MADRID.

Absolut ads
Posters from the long-running ad campaign in which a playful visual link is made between the shape of the Absolut vodka bottle and a major city.

Project

Produce posters for the next Olympic Games.

Project

Produce adverts for the next FIFA World Cup.

Project

Create an Absolut Vodka ad for your hometown. You will need to identify which building, product, activity or place best encapsulates it, then transform this into the shape of the Absolut bottle.

Make leaping jumps

In Make 'em Laugh (page 71) and Find a Link (page 82) you were challenged to make connections between words and between images. To do this you need to 'jump from one riverbank to another'.

This is a French expression that, applied to new and exciting ideas, neatly encapsulates the fact that leaps of thought are necessary to successfully link one thing to another. The creative thinker possesses a developed ability to make such jumps, and is also constantly on the lookout for new and undiscovered links between things.

Banana Nazis (left)
A swastika made from a discarded banana skin becomes a metaphor for the dangers of fascism.

Visual metaphors (opposite)
A shared dessert conveys equality, the fleetingness of life is reflected by a clock drawn on the rings of a tree stump, and the complications of love are represented by a prickly hearted cactus.

Project

Jump from one riverbank to another by spotting visual metaphors – objects that possesses the quality of something else. For example, a kite stuck in a tree is a metaphor for thwarted ambition, and a tangled knot is a metaphor for a very difficult problem.

The Greek philosopher Aristotle understood that making such leaping jumps was a key to creative thinking: 'The greatest thing by far is to be a master of metaphor.'

Project

Compile a playlist of songs for a party for textile designers. Some suggestions; 'Material Girl', anything by The Velvet Underground or The White Stripes, polkas, and the *Patton: Lust for Glory* theme. Then compile a playlist of songs for parties for the following: photographers, artists, engineers, florists, chefs, car salespeople.

Project

Play the Word Association Football Game, inspired by a John Cleese Monty Python sketch. In pairs or a group, take turns to exchange words. At each turn players should seek to make a leaping jump by considering all the contexts, uses and possibilities of the previous word. For example: Hot, curry, favour, party, labour, birth, cruise, Tom, cat, fat, bacon, Kevin, talk, force, air, son, rain, queen, ace, pilot, boiler, plot, and so on.

Fuck Ivy
A leaping jump could make this the start of an idea for this year's Christmas card.

Fail towards success

Successful creative businesses and leading art and design schools try to foster an environment and ethos that encourages and supports risk-taking and failure. In education this flies in the face of trends demanding institutions be formulaic and quantifiable.

The best schools nurture an atmosphere of daring, in which magnificent failure is applauded – understanding that taking chances, making mistakes, breaking rules and getting it totally wrong can all lead to discovery, new ways of thinking and great ideas.

In his book *Brilliant Blunders*, writer Mario Livio outlines how the mistakes of leading scientists – including Darwin, Kelvin and Einstein – led to the discovery of the ideas that shape our understanding of the world today.

Inventor Thomas Edison understood that failures are part of the process of discovery. He went through around 10,000 prototypes of the light bulb before getting it right. Instead of being dismayed and discouraged by this colossal failure rate he famously declared, 'I have not failed once. I have succeeded in proving that those 10,000 ways will not work. When I have eliminated the ways that will not work, I will find the way that will work.'

'Failing is one of the greatest arts in the world. We fail towards success.'

Charles Kettering, prolific inventor and pioneer of solar energy

'Nine out of ten of my experiments fail, and that is considered a pretty good record amongst scientists.'

Harold Kroto, Nobel prize-winning scientist

'An essential aspect of creativity is not being afraid to fail.'

Edwin Land, inventor of the Polaroid camera

'Ever tried. Ever Failed. No Matter. Fail again. Fail better.'

Samuel Beckett, writer

'An art college is a place to experiment, a place of unique freedom, a place to get it wrong, to make mistakes.'

Grayson Perry, artist

Projects

Using Edison's process of discovery through failure, find the maximum distance you can propel a piece of card or paper. You may only use basic materials.

Now discover the maximum time you can propel a piece of card or paper through the air before it hits the ground.

Propelling ideas
Students fail their way to success by creating and testing prototypes.

Find an analogy

Finding analogies can lead to new thinking and breakthroughs. An analogy is something that is comparable to something else. You can find an analogy by asking yourself, 'What is this like?', or 'In what situations has this problem been solved before?'

Engineer Marc Isambard Brunel, (father of the more famous Isambard Kingdom Brunel, *see also* page 53) discovered the perfect method for tunnelling through mud and clay to build the Thames Tunnel under London by observing the action of the shipworm, which tunnels through the hulls of boats, lining the hole with a hard chalky material as it goes. Mirroring the worm's action, Brunel designed a revolutionary and ingenious tunnelling system, in which workers could simultaneous cut and line a tunnel with brickwork to seal it. (*See also* Find Your Ingenious Inner Genius, page 66).

On its opening in 1843, the Thames Tunnel was described as the 'Eighth Wonder of the World', and Brunel's shipworm system is the basis of tunnelling methods still used today – a version of it was used in the construction of the 50-kilometre (31-mile) Channel Tunnel, built 40 metres (130 feet) below the seabed.

Thomas Heatherwick, Yorkshire Sound Barrier
Heatherwick made use of an analogy to design a barrier that would reduce traffic noise along a 2-kilometre (1¼-mile) stretch of motorway passing through a residential area in northern England. Knowing that egg boxes glued on to the walls of recording studios are used to dampen sound, he just needed to discover a large-scale equivalent – traffic cones. See www.heatherwick.com Heatherwick used traffic cones again to create a stunning entrance canopy for the 2012 exhibition of his work at London's V&A Museum. (Ask 'What Else Can I Do With This, page 58.)

....

'Where do ideas come from? From looking at one thing and seeing another.'

Saul Bass, designer

....

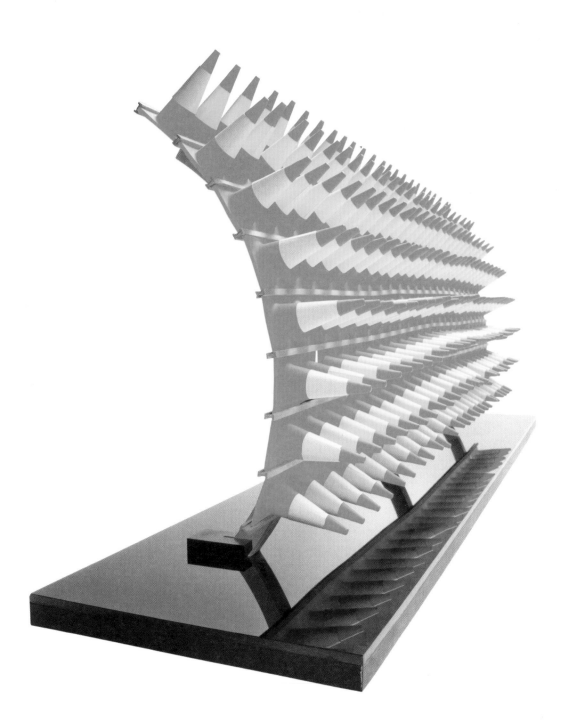

On seeing the action of a wine press, Johannes Gutenberg realized he had found the perfect mechanism to use for his idea from a printing press. Leonardo da Vinci designed a spiral staircase for the King of France based on the twisting internal form of the conch shell (*see also* Try Asking Nature, page 98). Harry Beck found that an electrical wiring diagram that expressed connections with great simplicity and precision was the perfect blueprint for his revolutionary London Underground map, whilst James Dyson found an analogy between the system used to suck up sawdust in sawmills and the home vacuum cleaner. (*See also* Try Swapping Systems, page 146, and Fix Your Frustrations, page 96.)

Analogous thinking

Asking 'In what situations has this problem been solved before?' can lead to solutions for many different challenges. As an example, see the paper prototypes on page 89. Analogous thinking in this situation leads to ideas for designs based on the objects we know can be thrown long distances, such as balls, frisbees, American footballs, javelins, darts and gliders, as well as methods used to project objects through the air, such as catapults and slingshots. It can also lead to ideas about the ways in which paper can leave the ground (designing paper kites, for example), and thoughts about which pieces of paper travel the furthest (resulting, in this case, in the ingenious winning solution of sticking a stamp on a bit of card and posting it to Australia).

Project

Find further visual analogies for the shape of a tent. What else is it like?

That's in-tents thinking
The 'Fully Booked', 'Earl of Sandwich' and 'What a Mellon' tents created by the English design company FieldCandy.

Change what appears to be fixed

New ideas flow when you break out of the rut of conventional or habitual thinking. One way of doing this is by seeking alternatives to the everyday things that we do and use – things that normally go totally unquestioned.

You can reinvent the wheel, part 1
Ron Arad's stunning 'Two Nuns' bike. Arad finds an alternative to the rubber tyres and spoked wheels that have been fixtures of bicycle design for over 100 years. See www.ronarad.co.uk
(*See also* You can reinvent the wheel, part 2, page 97.)

Identify the things that you take for granted and which seem fixed, then think of some alternatives. The more comprehensive your examination of what seems fixed, the more ideas you will come up with. Some of these will seem to lack sense or be unworkable. Some will be fun. Some will be absurd (*see also* Embrace Absurdity, page 136). Others will be ideas that somebody has already thought of. Some, though, will have great potential and possible application. Once you have ideas try combining them and yet more ideas will enter your mind.

The 'a' car electric taxi prototype (top)
James Moores and Dan Chadwick (pictured) changed almost everything that appears fixed about a taxi in the design and engineering of their highly innovative electric A-CAR. The wheels are very large (greatly improving the ride) and the body is symmetrical (greatly reducing cost). The driver also sits centrally. This both creates a tighter turning circle, and means that the vehicle can be sold all over the world. See www.danielchadwick.com

Plastic cars (above)
Cars rust, so why not make them from plastic instead? The rustproof plastic-panelled Citroën Méhari was designed by the French World War II flying ace Count Roland de la Poype, and produced for 20 years following its launch in 1968.

Example 1: What appears fixed about cars?

You drive: *alternative idea* – car drives itself. Cars have four wheels, two at the front, two at the rear: *alternative* – three, five or six wheels. Cars are parked horizontally: *alternative* – park cars vertically, then twice as many cars could be parked in cities. Old cars go to the scrapyard: *alternative* – design parts that have a future non-automotive use. You cannot change the colour of a car unless you pay for a highly expensive re-spray: *alternative* – a digital car body that can constantly change colour; additionally, this could display images or moving images. The front and rear of cars are different in design: *alternative* – design front and rear to be identical, thereby reducing manufacturing costs. Spare tyres are always tough to get to, and car bumpers crush when bumped: *alternative* – easy-release spare tyres that double as a rubbery back bumper. The engine is mounted at the front: *alternative* – mount the engine sideways. Alec Issigonis thought of this one for the Mini, which went on to sell millions (*see also* Visualize It, page 44).

Example 2: What appears fixed about eating in a café or restaurant?

They serve food: *alternative* – bring your own food. Bring your own ingredients and a chef cooks them for you; it's a 'take in' rather than a 'take away'. A chef cooks food for you: *alternative* – you cook your own food. Waiters bring food to your table: *alternatives* – you serve yourself. You serve other diners. Food comes to you by conveyor belt. Your order descends or ascends to your table. A drone delivers your food. The kitchen is out of sight: *alternative* – chefs and cooking are the central feature. You select your food from a menu: *alternative* – the chef selects your food; it's a surprise restaurant. The sequence of eating is fixed, with starters, main course, dessert: *alternatives* – serve a meal of 100 courses, as seen at Ferran Adrià's extraordinary El Bulli restaurant. Serve just starters, in a restaurant called Starters Orders. Just mains, in a restaurant called The Main Event. A café called Just Desserts. Diners sit at separate tables: *alternatives* – communal tables. A standing-only restaurant. You pay the bill: *alternative* – pay what you think the meal was worth. Pay per minute for the time you are there. Sing for your supper.

Project

Try changing what's fixed about a house.

Try changing what's fixed about a camera.

Fix your frustrations

Frustrations call out for new ideas and creative thinking to fix them. Frustrated that his garden wheelbarrow stuck in mud and that his vacuum cleaner quickly lost suction, inventor James Dyson decided to do something about them. Fixing these frustrations led to the innovative Ballbarrow and the bagless cyclone vacuum.

Dominic Wilcox, Finger Nose Stylus
Frustrated that wet fingers don't work for touchscreen navigation, Wilcox decided to do take action – inventing the bath-friendly Finger Nose Stylus. See dominicwilcox.com

Another of Dyson's inventions – the Airblade hand dryer – fixed everyone's frustration that electronic washroom hand dryers failed to ever dry your hands properly. Spotting frustrations or those moments in life when you feel 'I could design this better myself' can expose objects, systems and structures that are poorly designed, could be improved or simply don't work.

Who isn't frustrated whilst waiting for interminably slow lights to change at road junctions and pedestrian crossings? Some countries have fixed this frustration by having signals that count down the seconds before cars or pedestrians can proceed. This has proved a lifesaver, reducing the incidence of injury caused to those tempted to jump the lights. Another example is the 'turn on red' idea – where cars, motorbikes and bicycles in North America, the Middle East and Germany are permitted to turn right at red signals if the road

'Great ideas are often spurred on by an obsession to improve things that don't work properly.'
James Dyson, inventor

'The thing that has always driven me as a designer is feeling pissed off by the shitty stuff around me and wanting to make it better.'
Marc Newson, designer

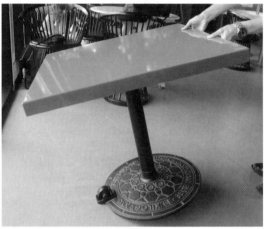

9.15 Fair Play vanishing spray (left)
In action at the 2014 World Cup.

Tom Dixon, 'Roll' table (below left)
Seeing restaurant staff struggling to move heavy tables spurred Dixon to create this dining table with a rolling wheel on the base, which enables it to be moved easily by one person. See www.tomdixon.net

You can reinvent the wheel, part 2 (below)
James Dyson's Ballbarrow. (*See also* You Can Reinvent the Wheel, part 1, page 93.)

is clear. As well as relieving the frustrations of drivers, this leads to reduced journey times and reduced emissions caused by needless idling.

Identify daily frustrations. Think of things that really make you fume. If something frustrates you it may well frustrate other people – a solution could be a breakthrough for all.

Pablo Silva tells of how he invented the spray used by officials to mark the line over which football players may not cross after he became frustrated by defenders encroaching as he tried to take a free-kick during a park match. "I was raging, ran to the referee and he showed me a red card. That's when I worked it out." The beautifully simple answer that fixed his frustration was developed with Fernando Martinez and Heine Allemagne.

Project

....

Try fixing the following frustrations:

'I get frustrated during those 20 minutes hanging around the luggage carousel, waiting for my baggage to come off the plane.'

'The petrol cap on my car always seems to be on the wrong side of the car when I get to a free pump.'

'I can never remember the ideas I had in the night.'

Try asking nature

The extraordinary challenges thrown at plants and animals by predators and climate elicit amazing examples of adaptation of shape, form and behaviour to aid survival. Let the outstanding creativity found in nature inspire new ideas.

Nature's prototypes

The incredible ways in which different plants and animals have learnt to fly, swim, walk, dive, navigate, communicate, build homes, take shelter, retain heat, keep cool, attract, repel, attack, defend and protect themselves, devour food, store food, raise young, absorb water, repel water, store water, camouflage themselves, and survive fire, frost and flood offer man innumerable readymade blueprints and prototypes for further development. László Moholy-Nagy, the Hungarian painter, photographer and teacher, advised his students to be inspired by such wondrous things and to use 'nature as a constructional model'.

If cockroaches are the only creatures that have a chance of surviving nuclear war, what can we learn from them that might give us a chance too?

'Evolution is the ultimate designer. It addresses issues of function, beauty, economy and sustainability. Nature has solved all these problems over time and is a great source of inspiration.'

John Makepeace, furniture designer

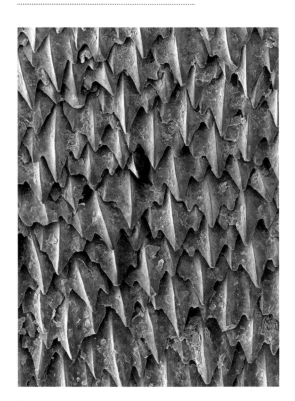

Natural problem solving
Designers at Speedo found a constructional model in the tiny tooth-like network found on the surface of a shark's skin. Called denticles (greatly magnified, above), these teeth reduce turbulence in water. Swimmers wearing the swimsuits bearing the resulting pattern won the vast majority of gold medals at the 2000 Olympic Games, breaking 13 out of 15 world records.

Massoud Hassani, tumbleweed toy
As a child, Massoud Hassani was inspired to create breeze-borne tumbling toys from scraps of material. These toys would often be blown into a nearby desert where retrieving them was impossible – it was a minefield.

How would this be solved by nature?

Got a problem? Ask how nature would solve it. Look at the engineering, structure, aesthetics and group organization present in nature; its efficiency and the systems whereby the waste from one thing nourishes others; and its symbiotic behaviour, in which entirely different species team up for mutual benefit.

Watch natural world documentaries – anything made by David Attenborough – all packed with nature's inspiring and often surprising adaptations.

Massoud Hassani, Mine Kafon mine exploder

As a design student Hassani came up with a brilliant way to get rid of the mines. Inspired by his tumbleweed toys he created the Mine Kafon, a low-cost, wind-powered mine exploder made mostly of bamboo, plastic and iron. Measuring over 2 metres (6½ feet) across and weighing 90 kilograms (200 pounds) it is heavy enough to trigger the mines, yet still light enough to be blown by the wind.

'You could look at nature as being like a catalogue of products, and all of those have benefited from a 3.8-billion-year research and development period.'

Michael Pawlyn, architect of the Eden Project

Project

Ask yourself: 'How would nature do it?'

Q. How can I promote a concert by a new band?
A. Try some of the numerous ways messages are spread in the natural world.

Q. How can I make clothing that is both protective and very lightweight?
A. Examine the structures of highly armoured insects.

Q. How can I regularly change the colour of my car?
A. Look at how snakes shed their skins, crabs change their shells, and chameleons and squid instantly alter their colour in response to their surroundings.

Change the room

A handful of remarkable buildings – including Bell Laboratories (Bell Labs), the Bauhaus, Lockheed's Skunk Works and the Brill Building – have been the birthplace of more innovative ideas per square metre than acres and acres of other workplaces put together.

In America their fame is such that Bell Labs has become a byword for scientific innovation and creativity, while 'The Skunk Works' has become a nickname for any highly creative group within an organization. The world's most creative addresses offer a set of blueprints for configuring and organizing places to make them particularly conducive to new ideas.

Set the house rules

Establishing how people act as individuals and together is more important than anything else. A set of house rules – an expectation of outlook and behaviour once the threshold has been crossed – can act as a very powerful creative catalyst. At Bell Labs, staff were given free rein to work on any problem that interested them. The only requirement was to keep an open door, so if anyone from another department came with a problem they would help to think about it. Bell Labs has been described as 'the ideas factory' and 'a legendary playpen' (see Be Playful, page 10). Permission should be granted to make a mess, make mistakes and break rules. The house rules of ad agency BBH in London

are signalled by the life-size sculpture of a black sheep at the entrance, indicating that this is a place for out-of-the-ordinary and disreputable thinking.

Maximize interaction

Spaces should be designed to allow knowledge to be shared freely, and to ensure exposure to the ideas of others is unavoidable. In the Brill Building, teams of young songwriters worked in adjoining rooms. Paper-thin walls meant each could hear how the others were progressing, allowing ideas to permeate.

Grant ownership

A shared happy memory of art students of earlier generations was that they were allowed keys to their college studios to work undisturbed whenever they wanted – overnight or through weekends or holidays. Giving ownership of an establishment's space frees individuals mentally and physically to pursue and evolve their ideas far beyond nine-to-five constraints.

Flexible space
An ingenious see-through room within a room at the London Design Festival, created with just coloured string by B&O.

'High achievement always takes place in the framework of high expectation.'

Charles Kettering, inventor and pioneer of solar energy

'The right environment can immediately liberate creative potential – when conversations are taking place, work is on the walls and there is an atmosphere of ambition and endeavour you feel you're in a space where anything is possible.'

John Myerson, advertising teacher

All in the same room
A creative studio at the University of Gloucestershire. Its walls on wheels, towers, screens and blackout blinds mean it can be reconfigured in seconds.

Go reconfigure

Ideas environments should be the visual embodiment of creativity. They should offer maximum flexibility rather than permanence – spaces that can be reconfigured swiftly for different activities, offering opportunities to continually surprise. One designer who worked for Charles and Ray Eames described that entering their studios in California 'was like walking into a circus. If you could take the roof off you would see it constantly changing.'

Get a ringleader

'Every place needs a fireball or sparkplug' said one former Skunk worker; theirs was legendary creative leader Clarence 'Kelly' Johnson. A ringleader must be respected, believed in and seen as representing the collective good. The best have the ability to encourage and energize without dominating – their role is to move things on, to influence by drawing ideas together, be the play-maker, keeping the competition going, and help to draw conclusions. The most successful managers and coaches in the creative field of sport share very similar attributes. José Mourinho reflected that his success was due to an 'accepted leadership'.

'There is a set of conditions that great ringleaders in design construct in the minds of those they work with. The key thing they do is to make everyone feel simultaneously secure but challenged. These things seem oppositional to start with. Things mustn't be too settled or cosy – that causes people to revert to imitation. Everyone needs to know and feel that they're not going to be tested, 'marked down' or ridiculed. There has to be a respectful relationship with the ringleader – that means people can then start to make mistakes. If you don't establish that two-way trust, you can't ask people to step out of line, you can't ask people to try things that may not work. Everyone must feel that whatever they come up with is valuable.'

Nick Pride, designer and design teacher

Projects

Reconfigure your creative zone.

Create a written code of conduct for your own ideas-seeking space.

Gaining ownership
These Chinese art students were
encouraged to take ownership of their
brand new building through projects that
made creative use of the windows, walls
and front doors.

Build your own space

New ideas sometimes occur or are developed with the stimulus of periods of interaction with others – see Get Help, page 49, and Change the Room, page 102. Equally important, though, is the need for time alone.

Having a place in which to be alone is vital to the process of thinking, both in a concentrated manner and in the opposite way – by letting the mind wander. Having your own space offers freedom: the freedom to make progress at your own pace and to experiment, make a mess and make mistakes without fear of intervention or criticism by others. A private, secluded space – even in a communal environment – is necessary to form and shape your thoughts.

Build a retreat from the outside world

Studios, studies and sheds should be sanctuaries and are the choice of many for periods of working alone. They are private places for obsessions and obsessiveness. Once immersed in your own world you can feel free from the normal rules, conventions, formalities and hierarchies of the nine-to-five world outside. Writer Roald Dahl made his personal creative space in a shed in his garden – no one was allowed to enter except him. He described his transformation upon entering: 'You become a different person; you are no longer an ordinary fellow who walks around and looks after his children and eats meals and does silly things, you go into a completely different world' (*see also* page 34).

Make a hands-on space – surround yourself with tools

Proximity to tools and materials, coupled with the process of exploration and experiment, can give you new ideas and also help to develop the ones you already have in your head. A space for making ideas tangible is key to creativity. Getting thoughts from your head into a visible form through experimentation, prototyping and trial and error is a vital part of the evolution of ideas. (*See also* Be Playful, page 10, and Visualize It, page 44.)

Francis Bacon, at 7 Reece Mews, London (opposite)
Bacon's studio was notorious for its mess. It was piled high with paints, brushes, books, drawings, slashed canvases and torn photographs, and its walls were smeared with paint. It was the birthplace of some of the greatest paintings of the 20th century.

Studio portraits
Artists Ron Mueck and Peter Davies, photographed in their studios by Johnnie Shand Kydd.

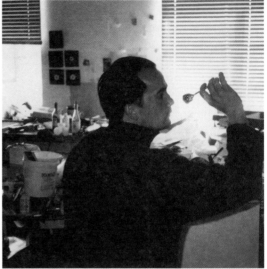

Studio portraits, continued
Sarah Lucas, Mark Francis and Fiona Rae,
photographed in their studios by Johnnie
Shand Kydd.

Project

Explore the private spaces of your creative
heroes and heroines; there are many
websites and books of photographs that
will allow you entry. See, for example, the
writer George Bernard Shaw's sanctuary –
a hut in his garden that revolved to follow
the sun, allowing it to always be flooded
with light.

Try osmosis

Emptiness and sterility are not conducive to ideas. By boldly surrounding yourself with influences – things you are curious about, the work of your heroes, the innovators in your field, and historic and contemporary imagery – you make yourself open to ideas by osmosis, the process of gradual, often unconscious absorption.

Poet Dylan Thomas described his creative place (a hut in his garden) as 'wordsplashed', as it was pasted with clippings of the writing of his literary heroes – Lord Byron, Walt Whitman, W. H. Auden and William Blake.

While it's important to see the work of others, it's equally important to see your own work and things that have special meaning for you. Creating your own Aladdin's cave – a space rich with ephemera, objects, collections and mementoes can provide great inspiration, as unique stories, history and memories are embedded in these personal possessions.

A wall of faces
Pictures torn from magazines provide inspiration for the artist Nigel Langford's paintings.

Teacher and designer Nick Pride said of such special places: 'Every day you come into that space those images talk back to you; they are the foundation on which you build your work. Below the conscious level the mind is continuously scanning them for possibilities and making fresh connections.'

If you are open to these influences, ideas will come to you.

Inspiration through osmosis (left and opposite)
The studios of illustration and painting students at the University of Gloucestershire are filled with possessions, experiments and works-in-progress.

Project

....

Word splash and picture splash your space.

Change the scenery

Travelling boosts the ability to think creatively. In addition to being physically somewhere different, the mind is also transported to new places.

There are almost 200 countries in the world, each with different ways of doing things, and whilst abroad you frequently encounter the mind-opening experience of seeing things that have been solved much better than they have at home. With this comes the accompanying revelation that other perspectives and viewpoints are available, even with the things we imagine are fixed. In Japanese airports, for example, the luggage trolleys can travel up and down escalators, and on the bullet trains every chair swivels so that passengers can reconfigure seating to suit their own preference.

As a stranger in a new environment, everything is fresh and exciting; you see things with a clarity and intensity rarely experienced at home. Whilst travelling in Asia, designer John Firewater wrote: 'It's amazing how many new things you spot. It's freezing here, minus five. I noticed that when getting on buses that have no heating, leaky windows and are pretty much as cold as outside, everyone takes their gloves off. I thought this was a show of local hardiness – but no – it's so that when the bus lurches to a halt or veers suddenly to avoid potholes you can grip the metal poles and avoid injury. Hey, someone needs to design better gloves or better poles.'

Revolutionary idea, 1
Revolving seats on Japanese bullet trains allow passengers to choose how their carriage is configured.

Revolutionary idea, 2
Parking turntables in Tokyo.

If you can't physically travel, change the scenery by voyaging in your imagination with the help of foreign films, books and museums. Placing yourself in a traveller's mindset can promote fresh thinking. As writer Walter Benjamin recommended, 'Walk out of your front door as if you've just arrived from a foreign country; to discover the world in which you already live; to begin the day as if you've just gotten off the boat from Singapore and have never seen your own door mat.'

Just improvise

The ability to improvise is an approach to problem solving that views the resources at hand as the perfect components with which to assemble a solution. Its on-the-spot designing – you have to work with what you've got.

Improvisation is against-the-odds creativity. It is a way of thinking and acting that can lead to solutions in hugely challenging situations – when people find themselves imprisoned, cast away, stranded, besieged, trapped, fenced in, lost at sea, capsized or shipwrecked.

Some acts of improvisation are legendary – using tights to replace a car's broken fan belt is perhaps an urban myth, although British spy George Blake did escape from prison using a rope ladder whose 20 rungs were made from size 13 knitting needles. Many books and films centre on feats of improvisation – some fact, some fiction – including *Robinson Crusoe*, *The Great Escape* and *Apollo 13*. Comedians can demonstrate great verbal improvisation in live performance by escaping from staged tasks or from audience heckles. The audience's pleasure is derived from witnessing the comic get off the hook and cleverly triumph over adversity. Musical improvisation is a similar high-wire act.

Allora & Calzadilla, *Under Discussion*, 2005, video still (above)
Great improvisers can turn the tables on any problem.

Using found objects
An improvised sledge (opposite top) and improvised instruments (middle).

Farmyard improvisation (opposite bottom)
Farmers are notorious improvisers, with orange baler twine being by far their most favoured material – using it to mend, attach, pull, lasso, hold up, hold down and, as here, fasten a jacket with a broken zip. *Farmers Weekly* magazine once ran a great April Fool's Day article, predicting the collapse of British farming due to a baler twine shortage.

Project

The design miles challenge: The 'food miles' initiative questioned the vast distances much food had travelled from its point of production to the dinner table. The campaign advocated choosing local produce, which, having travelled the least distance, depleted fewer of the world's resources. The 'design miles' challenge is similar. Only use what is very close at hand – challenge yourself to solve problems using only what is in your pockets, on the table, freely available, left over from another job, or only what is within a very short distance.

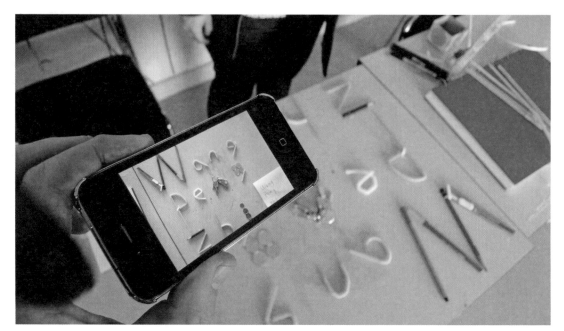

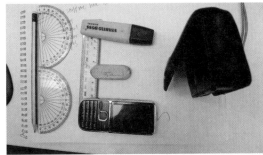

Improvised names

Students improvise their own names
– Wang Peng Zhi, Jake, Yasmin, Wang,
Shay, Tim, Jenny, Ben, Lawrence and
James – using only things immediately
at hand.

Go to the factory

Ideas can come from seeing how things are made. Investigating the processes of production and manufacture – the things that many leave to others – can lead to breakthroughs. Visit factories, manufacturers, producers, constructors, suppliers, printers, labs, and so on.

Talk to people about each process and method. Talk to the experts – the makers, the repairers and the people who dispose of products at the end of their lifespan. Look for things that have been rejected – investigate what is in the bins and skips, ready for recycling, thrown out or leaning against a wall. Find the misprints and mistakes, overprints, rejects, tests, the bits cut off in finishing; these can reveal ideas from which you can build new things.

Always ask why things are done as they are – often the answer is that it's cheap or quick, 'That's how we always do it', or 'No one has ever asked for it to be done differently.' Questioning invariably leads to alternatives: magazine editor László József Bíró became fascinated by the quick-drying ink he'd come across at his printers; whilst thinking of other uses for it he came up with the idea for the ballpoint pen.

'I'm very excited by factories and the way things are made. Quite often things don't exist in your mind until you've been to see a place where you can make it.'

Tom Dixon, designer

Instrumental thinking (opposite)
Artist and designer Mark Unsworth
found the perfect material to assemble
this music poster in the bin – curvaceous
pieces of wood left over from laser
cutting that collectively brought to mind
the abstracted shapes of instruments.

Factory visits
Visits to (clockwise from below) a
machinist, sandblaster, laser cutter,
scrapyard, timberyard, steelyard and
a studio can provide great inspiration.

121

Project

Develop designs based on the discoveries you make on a factory visit.

Trust your hunches

During the process of trying to solve a challenge we sometimes experience a spontaneous and unstoppable inner conviction to proceed in a certain direction. This often swiftly passing twinge – in which we sense we know what to do but don't know why – has been described as 'a hunch', 'intuition', 'instinct', 'a sixth sense, 'a feeling in my bones' or 'a gut reaction'. Never, ever ignore it.

It has been suggested that this feeling is caused by a subconscious recognition in the mind that a problem fits a pattern it's come across before, and therefore knows what to do without you ever consciously seeing or understanding the resemblance. Your mind has instantly leapt across to a riverbank without you realizing. As film director Frank Capra said, 'a hunch is creativity trying to tell you something'. Always listen to this inner voice and develop your intuitive ideas.

And it may be that we really can think with our gut. We have neurons – the cells that gather and transmit information within our brains – embedded in the stomach and intestine walls; around 100 million of them.

Project

Ideas surface from intuitive hands-on experimentation with materials. Explore the potential of bamboo canes purchased from your local garden centre – let your intuition rise to the challenge and lead you. Try connecting your hunches.

Project

Collect and collate your intuitive ideas. Think of a title for this collection – designer David Carson named his 'Second Sight'.

Patrick Hughes, *Fear Itself*, 1984
Be aware of when your intuition is trying
to guide you. Ignore it at your peril.

Potter, ponder and tinker

Many strategies focus on plans of action to catalyze ideas. Taking the opposite approach can be equally effective. Setting out purposefully without aim or plan and heading off in an unknown direction without an end result, brief or client in mind can lead to discoveries.

Words describing this form of working include 'pottering' and 'tinkering' – activities that allow insights, realization and direction to surface through the combination of tools, time and figuring things out by trial and error.

This method of discovery is joyous, combining an open mind with getting your hands dirty. It can often lead to pet projects – personal adventures in developing your own ideas.

Further viewing

See work by Tinkering School, the educational programme founded in California by the writer and computer scientist Gever Tulley: www.tinkeringschool.com

Instrumental thinking
Tinkering with broken scanners and cameras led these photography students to discover exciting new ways of recording the world.

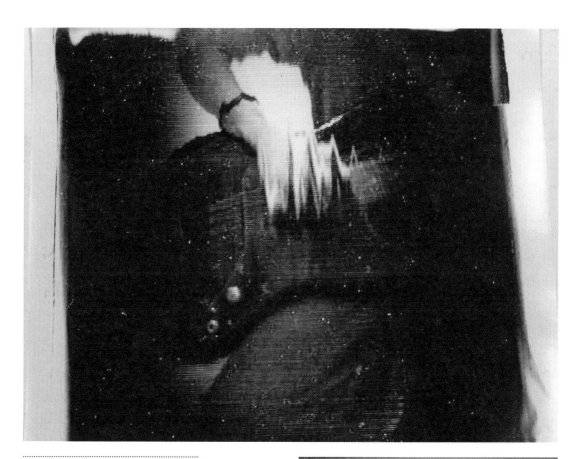

'When I was young, I loved to take things apart. Our home was littered with the dismembered remains of toasters, radios, turntables and batteries. At some point, I managed to reassemble them in working order. An engineering career seemed inevitable. For me, breaking stuff is the step[ping] stone to making stuff. Tinkering gives you the design instinct and applied knowledge that's hard to get any other way.'

Ralph Oei, design writer and editor

Project

Head in an unknown direction to discover the possibilities of a broken camera.

Try translating

Ideas are greatly stimulated by the process of translation. Converting things from one form or medium into another can guide thoughts in totally new and exciting directions. One idea leads to another – and then you're off on the ideas trail.

The Russian artist Wassily Kandinsky translated Classical music into abstract paintings, selecting different colours to signify the varying emotions the music provoked. He also invented a machine that translated musical sounds into instructions for paintings.

Purposefully engaging the imagination by translating thoughts, ideas and problems into different forms or languages can lead to new discoveries, understandings and ways of communicating.

Translating letters into costumes
Chinese art students translate letterforms into costumes for a typography party.

Project

Translate the following words into drawings – triangle, square, hot, cold, ice, faster, slower.

Translate the following words into typography – lazy, happy, loud, soft.

Translate the following smells into drawings – ground coffee, fresh bread, the seaside.

Translate the following musical forms into images – jazz, rap, reggae, punk, Classical music.

Communicate to a friend the following cities through mime – New York, Paris, Sydney, Cairo, London.

Translate a series of words and phases into rebuses (pictures that are used to represent words, or parts of words).

Translating pictures into music (top)
Musician Ben Hough translates the position of a flock of birds perched on telephone wires into a composition.

Translating words and phrases into images (above)
Words, phrases and messages that are created solely through images have the advantage of being globally understood.

Sleep on it

Our imaginations are particularly powerful during sleep. During these hours they go to work dreaming up ideas. In dreams we think differently; our brains are unharnessed from daily routines and can rearrange, combine, condense and amplify things in a way that they rarely can when we are awake.

It is not uncommon to find ideas solidifying during sleep and to awake with a perfectly formed answer to a previously unsolved problem. The unconscious mind seems to enjoy working on the challenges unsolved by the conscious mind.

The moments just after falling asleep and just before waking seem to be highly creative times, perhaps because our brains are then at a midpoint between consciousness and unconsciousness. Inventor Thomas Edison was particularly interested in these brief junctures and ingeniously attempted to utilize them. He would sit in front of a fire when feeling sleepy, holding ball bearings in his hand. As he fell asleep, the ball bearings would drop to the ground, instantly waking him, at which point he would write down any ideas that he could remember. Artist Salvador Dalí is said to have used a similar technique with cutlery.

'At night while we are asleep our brains are secretly moonlighting for us.'

Rose Tang, artist

'We think that what's happening in sleep is that you open the aperture of memory and are able to see the bigger picture.'

Matthew Walker, neuroscientist

Project

Try out Edison's ball-bearing strategy.

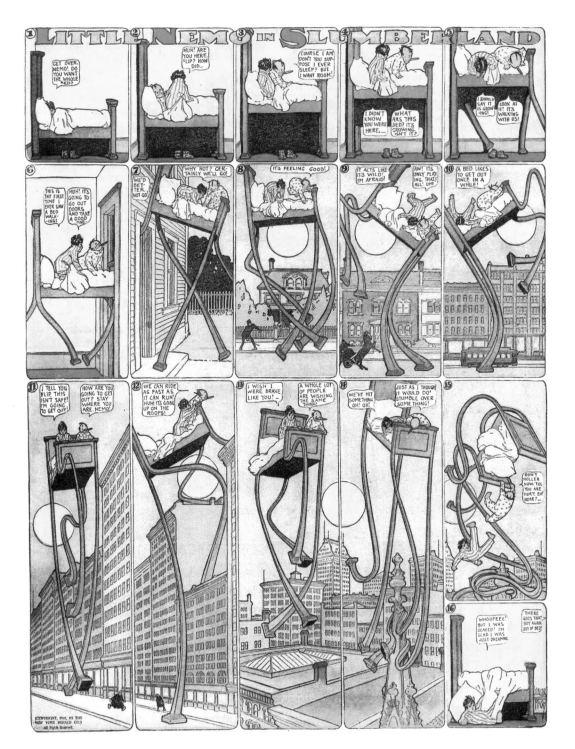

Winsor McCay, *Little Nemo in Slumberland*, 1909

The American artist Winsor McCay created wonderful depictions of the highly imaginative world we enter during sleep in his long-running Little Nemo series. Similar representations of dreaming make for some of the most memorable moments in cinema history – see, for example, *The Wizard of Oz*, the sequence Salvador Dalí created for Alfred Hitchcock's *Spellbound*, and the dream sequences in *The Big Lebowski* and Terry Gilliam's *Brazil*.

Take a break

Taking a break from actively trying to find answers to a challenge can be the key to solving it. This is counterintuitive – appearing to be the opposite of what common sense indicates – but time after time, when you stop thinking about a problem and do something else you find ideas.

By letting go and doing something that you find enjoyable, such as walking, reading or listening to music, you move the problem from the front to the back of your mind, where another part of the imagination seems to happily pick up the challenge, getting to work whilst you think you've temporarily forgotten about it. Ensure, therefore, that you include relaxation time as part of your creative process. (See Understand Your Process, page 176.)

Go for a drive

Driving seems to unlock ideas for many people. One designer interviewed for this book realized that her ideas always seem to gel at a particular set of traffic lights on the school run.

'When I am, as it were, completely myself, entirely alone, and of good cheer – say travelling in a carriage, or walking after a good lunch, or during the night when I cannot sleep: it is on such occasions that my ideas flow best and most abundantly.'

Extract from a letter by composer Wolfgang Amadeus Mozart, c.1789

'The best ideas, the most creative thoughts come to you when you're not thinking. There is a really important aspect of our week which we forget about – the time when we are doing nothing.'

Gavin Pretor-Pinney, author and founder of the Cloud Appreciation Society

Marcel Duchamp by Man Ray, 1919
Taking a break is just as important as actively striving for answers in the ideas-seeking process.

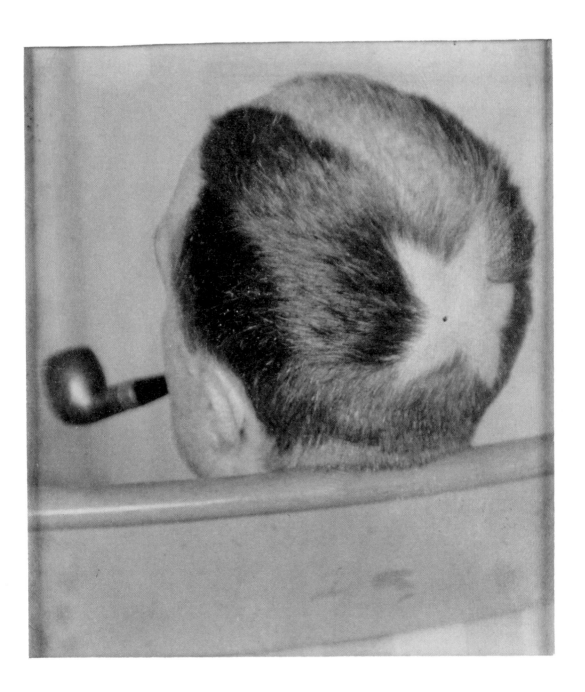

'I've found all my good ideas come when I'm very relaxed […] I was on a beach on Bournemouth walking along with my wife when the idea suddenly came to me.'

Alf Adams, physicist discussing the moment he had the idea for the lasers that power the internet, computer mice, DVDs, CDs and supermarket scanners

'Your subconscious is really getting to work on stuff […] your best ideas come to you when you are walking or when you are not thinking about the idea. Your subconscious is this huge glacial thing under the water that is doing a lot of work when you don't realize it.'

Graham Linehan, writer of TV comedies *Father Ted* and *The IT Crowd*

'I get my best ideas in my car. In a car you can't do anything practical. So your thoughts start wandering off into a different mode. It's as if I'm working on two levels; I'm driving and at the same time I am somewhere else. Working out how to solve a problem always happens in my car.'

Lotte Romer, musician and author

'You know it's a great idea if you've had to stop the car to write it down.'

John Firewater, designer

'Stuff your conscious mind with information, then unhook your rational thought process. You can help this process by going for a long walk, or taking a hot bath, or drinking half a pint of claret. Suddenly, if the telephone line from you unconscious is open, a big idea wells up within you.'

David Ogilvy, adman

Project

Do something else – relax. Experiment with different balances of time between actively working and taking a break. Discover which relaxing activities work best for you. (*See also* Understand Your Process, page 176.)

Spend time daydreaming

Daydreaming is a particularly creative activity that is often foolishly frowned upon by teachers and bosses. In daydreams the mind wanders in a freethinking way, without method, logic or purpose.

'What do clouds see when they daydream?'

Taika Waititi, film director, writer, painter, comedian and actor

'Who cannot remember looking and finding shapes in the clouds when they were kids – when we were masters of daydreaming […] as adults we are reluctant to allow our imaginations to drift along in the breeze […] we should live with our head in the clouds now and then.'

Gavin Pretor-Pinney, author and founder of the Cloud Appreciation Society

These lapses of concentration where all focus is lost are times when our brains seem incredibly playful, spontaneous, free and uncensored, and able to make associations and connections inaccessible through other means. Jonah Lehrer, writer for the *New Yorker*, wrote: 'A daydream is that fountain spurting, spilling strange new thoughts into the stream of consciousness.'

'Daydreaming allows the mind to come up with ideas […] my radio idea was prompted by a television programme about HIV and AIDS in Africa, which said that disease could only be prevented by the spread of information, but there was no electricity or batteries. I started daydreaming about the way old-fashioned wind-up gramophones worked and it all went from there.'

Trevor Baylis, inventor of the wind-up radio

Project

In our digital age there seems little opportunity for daydreaming activity as so many things have to be viewed, answered and updated. Make time to get your head in the clouds and photograph the new things you find.

Embrace absurdity

Absurdity is at the heart of some of the most creative ideas of the nineteenth and twentieth centuries. Lewis Carroll and Edward Lear used absurdity in storytelling; the Marx Brothers, Spike Milligan and Monty Python exploited it as a source of comedy; Samuel Beckett used it for drama; Elsa Schiaparelli in fashion design; Frank Zappa for music; and the Dadaists and Surrealists used it to make art.

**Nina Saunders, *Exhale*, 2007
(opposite)**
Strange and startling collisions feature in
the wonderful work of this Danish artist.
See www.ninasaunders.eu

**Markus Hofer, *Tour de la realité*, 2010
(below)**
Austrian artist Hofer plumbs a bicycle
to the wall, making an irreconcilable
connection. See www.markushofer.at

Absurd ideas suspend the rules and certainties
of logic and the rational world, replacing them
with nonsensicality, ambiguity and the irrational.
They frequently feature strange meetings of
wildly incongruous things – for example, a
'chance encounter between a sewing machine
and an umbrella on a dissecting table'. This is a
line from the poetry by the nineteenth-century
godfather of absurdity, French writer Isidore-
Lucien Ducasse, aka the Comte de Lautréamont
(see page 53).

*'I believe that in design, 30 per cent
dignity, 20 per cent beauty and 50
per cent absurdity are necessary.'*

Shigeo Fukuda, designer

*'The chief enemy of creativity
is "good" sense.'*

Pablo Picasso, artist

'To me, absurdity is the only reality.'

Frank Zappa, musician

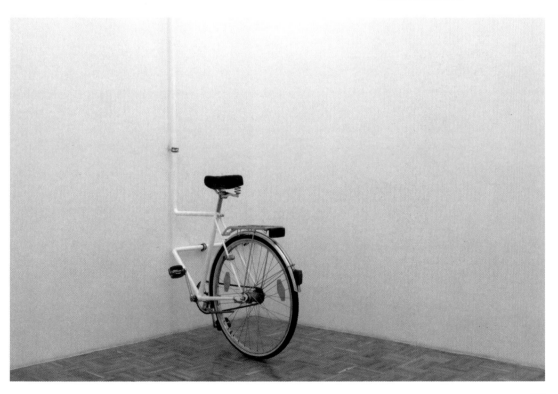

Elsa Schiaparelli, Shoe hat, 1937-38
Schipaparelli overturned the rational world by turning footwear into headwear in this famous collaboration with artist Salvador Dalí. It is now in the V&A Museum in London.

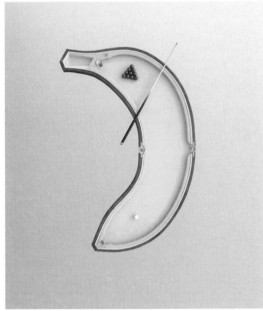

Cléon Daniel, *Corner Ladder* and *Banana Pool Table*
Artist and designer Daniel surprises with unfamiliar versions of familiar objects. See www.cleondaniel.com and Daniel's great book *Unventions*.

Absurd ideas have impact through their disconnectedness. No matter how hard we strive to connect the elements in our imaginations, they are still irreconcilable because they fail to adhere to traditional or familiar structures – although to be successful there should be a balance between the elements that intrigues, entertains or makes us think.

Embracing absurdity can lead to breakthrough ideas. Never reject the ideas you come up with that seem ridiculous or illogical – always fully consider them as possible solutions.

Project

Using the visual language of signage systems, create absurd signs that confound viewers, provoking thought or laughter.

Take a chance

Chance was a crucial creative strategy for Surrealist artists, writers and poets. They saw it as a way of releasing thinking from the constraints of the rational world, and found that it could produce images and text that rivalled the intensity of imagery normally found only in dreams.

Salvador Dalí, *The Temptation of Saint Anthony*, 1946
Dalí's work usually included dream-like imagery and strange juxtapositions.

Exquisite chance
The Surrealists frequently played the
game Exquisite Corpse (below) to
chance upon new ideas. The influence
of this approach can be seen in many of
the paintings of Salvador Dalí (opposite)
and Magritte (overleaf).

They often played drawing games relying on
chance, including Exquisite Corpse, in which
players take turns to draw the head, body
and feet of a person, concealing each part in
turn by folding over the paper before handing
it to the next person. Through chance, new
relationships are formed between each part
of the drawing; connections are revealed that
would be impossible to discover otherwise.
The Surrealists also played similar games
using collage and words – again, keeping each
addition hidden until the end of the game, then
using the results as starting points for paintings
and writing.

Similar chance strategies have been used by
artists, writers and musicians including William
Burroughs, David Bowie and Brion Gysin, who
sliced through layers of newspapers to discover
chance juxtapositions of words and images only
revealed by peeling the layers away.

Musician and artist John Cage (see page 172)
simply used to toss a coin to determine pitch,
duration and volume for some compositions.

....

'Make chance essential.'
Paul Klee, painter

....

Projects

Play Exquisite Corpse with drawings and words. Build from the things that chance brings.

Use the Surrealist method of mark-making called 'automatic drawing'. Began drawing on a sheet of paper with no preconceived subject or composition in mind, letting your pen or pencil travel rapidly without conscious control. After a couple of minutes hand it to a partner for them to complete by building on the things that chance has created. *See also* the automatic drawings of André Masson.

Play the 'word of the day' game.

Random thoughts

In his teachings on lateral thinking, Edward de Bono recommended randomly choosing a word from the dictionary as a method of driving thinking in new directions. A similar strategy has been used by ad agencies. Project manager Aya Abou-Taha recalls 'a random word of the day – the game was seeing how often we could sneak it into conversation, gossip, presentations and ideas for the projects we were working on. It worked brilliantly as a catalyst and it was amazing how often it led to new thinking.'

Fence yourself in

Constraints can make for creativity. Designer and writer on creativity Alan Fletcher said, 'The worst thing that anyone can say to me is "Do whatever you like". Then I have to set up my own boundaries, and fence myself in.'

Being fenced in – having a lack of choice – gives you something to fight against. Counter-intuitively, it makes ideas easier to come by as choices are simpler and the task is very clear – you know this is all you have to make it work.

The Photobooth Challenge (below and overleaf)
Responses by art students to the challenge to be creative within the constraints of a tiny photobooth.

Constraints and creative buildings

Interestingly, many highly creative concerns choose to locate themselves in old buildings converted to suit their purpose. There are numerous examples: the Eames's studio was in an old garage, Ron Arad's is in an old piano factory, London's Tate Modern is in an old power station. Having to work with the constraints of the existing configurations of rooms, walls, ceilings and proportions makes for far more dynamic and exciting spaces than many constructed from scratch.

Force creativity

Forcing yourself through boundaries can lead to much more creative solutions. Options are revealed by deliberately establishing some constraints for yourself (right):

Ask yourself ...

What would I do if I only had half of the existing budget?

What would I do if I had half the time to complete the challenge?

What would I do if I could only use off-the-shelf parts?

What would I do if I could only use bits I already have to assemble a solution?

What would I do if I was only allowed to use just 2, 4, 8 or 16 pieces?

What would I do if I had to work without a computer?

What would I do if I could only work with the very cheapest materials?

Project

The Photobooth Challenge: The high street or train station passport photobooth seems to offer little choice. It is concreted or bolted to the ground, a tiny cubicle with set lighting, a fixed lens with predetermined exposure, a white background, and a very tight field of view. Your challenge is to be creative within all these constraints.

Try swapping systems

Applying a readymade, successful, tried and trusted existing system from one area of practice to another can lead to great innovation.

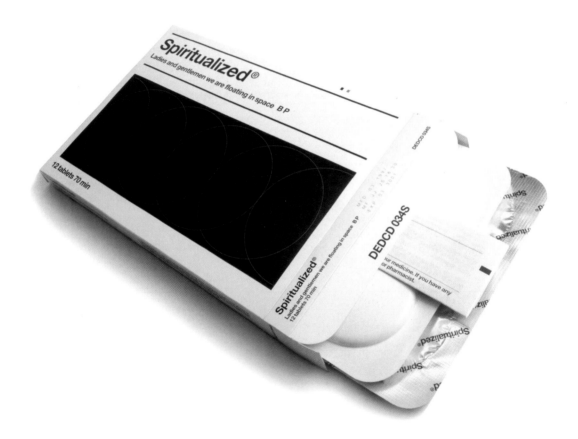

Applying pharmaceutical packaging to music

Farrow Design packaged the album *Ladies and Gentlemen We Are Floating in Space*, by Spirtualized, using a design system commonly found in pharmacies. Looking just like a box of prescription drugs, each 'pill blister' contained a CD that had to be popped through the foil before it could be played. The credits were printed as a medicine information sheet and contained warnings on the possible side effects of listening to the band. Farrow went on to package a later Spirtualized album using the typographic style of the Accident and Emergency departments found in UK hospitals. See www.farrowdesign.com

Applying property sales techniques to a design festival

An existing readymade system for printing and erecting estate agents' boards provided a highly original way to promote a highly original annual design festival.
See www.cheltenhamdesignfestival.com

Inventor Owen Maclaren created the first collapsible baby buggy by utilizing the system designed for the folding undercarriages of Spitfire fighter planes from World War II, while James Dyson used the cyclone systems used to suck up sawdust in sawmills and applied it to the home vacuum (*see also* Fix Your Frustrations, page 96). Both revolutionized previously entrenched designs. A spiral ramp might be fairly standard in an inner-city car park, but it is highly remarkable as an interior walkway of a public art gallery. If you find a current system disappointing or inadequate, try borrowing one from another field.

Project

Take the quick-change systems of theatre scenery and apply them to rethink your living or workspace.

Try combining systems

Exciting new ideas can come from bringing together and interlinking previously existing infrastructures and systems.

Lamp-posts combined with goal posts
Prize-winning designer Tom Jarvis moved the goal posts in his great idea for lighting urban playgrounds.

'Combinatory play seems to be the essential feature in productive thought.'

Albert Einstein, scientist

In Beijing metro stations you can pay for travel with empty plastic bottles, by means of a wonderful idea that combines the ticket machine system with a recycling bottle bank – who wouldn't want to use this?

Are you sick of waiting at home for parcels to be delivered? Why not have them sent to your local newsagent and collect them at your convenience? (*See also* Fix Your Frustrations, page 96.)

Both of these ideas bring seemingly distinct infrastructures together: in combination they are redefined, bring benefit and can gain appeal. Designer Robin Southgate's pop-up toaster, linked to online meteorological forecasts, is another great example – it predicts the day's weather for breakfasters by printing symbols for sunny, cloudy or rainy on their morning toast.

Combining recycling and public transport (above)
Paying for travel by recycling your waste.

Combining for good (right)
Simon Berry had the brilliant idea that lifesaving medicines could be freely distributed to far-flung areas of rural Africa by 'piggybacking' on an existing distribution system – that of Coca-Cola. The design of the Kit Yamoyo (Kit of Life) means it fits perfectly between the bottles within the crates.

New systems can also be combined with existing ones. To bring the new innovation of electric lighting into homes in the 1880s, wizard of invention Thomas Edison used existing gas pipes to carry wires through buildings, and placed bulbs in converted gas fixtures. Today, lifesaving water-purifying machines and medicines to treat common illnesses that cause child mortality are being distributed to remote areas of Africa using the long-established transport infrastructures of soft drinks companies (see page 149).

Instead of attempting to create completely new systems or infrastructures, look at existing products, appliances and common methods of delivery, purchase, transport, communication, dissemination of information and entertainment, and the possibilities for combination and interconnection.

Combining the technology of mobile phones with systems in the home also offers numerous new possibilities. Ideas developed in this area include innovative washing machines, smoke alarms and central heating systems.

Projects

Produce ideas for interlinking text messaging with photobooths, vending machines, watercoolers or video game machines.

What existing system can you link with the network of phone boxes to successfully bring them back into regular everyday use? One solution is seen the village of Glendaruel, Scotland, where a life-saving defibrillator has been installed in the local phone box. In other places, phone boxes have been repurposed as micro libraries.

Be a storyteller

Great stories take an audience on an exciting journey through a series of ideas that have been successfully interlinked. One-line jokes, 30-second TV ads, two-minute comedy sketches, three-minute pop songs and music videos, as well as graphic novels, plays, ballets, operas, movies, cartoons, graphic novels and video games, all rely on successful storytelling.

Book design, exhibition design, web design and magazine design at their best also engage by possessing an enveloping narrative. Photographers, too, strive to tell a story – in their case, in a single image in which all the parts are related. In fact, they even refer to this perfect intersection of the pieces as 'the storytelling moment'.

....

'Storytelling is the most powerful way to put ideas into the world.'

**Robert McKee,
writer and teacher**

....

'We are the storytelling animal.'

Salman Rushdie, writer

....

The Storyboard Game
Stories created by playing the Storyboard Game, in which participants take turns to begin, evolve and complete stories.

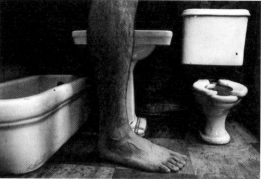

Duane Michals, *Things Are Queer*, 1973
An amazing cyclical story, perfectly
planned and executed by the artist
and photographer Michals.

A story needs to grab an audience, ambush their imaginations and transport them to another place; the finest do this through immersing the reader, listener, viewer or, in the case of video games, the player, in the unique worldview of the teller by employing a highly distinctive voice or vision.

Great stories feel highly personal – the ideas they contain speak to you by engaging your thoughts or emotions, through recognition or through empathy. Film director Danny Boyle has described this phenomenon as 'a perfect vacuum', where there is 'nothing between you and the story'.

Street View stories
Artists Dan Glaister and Ali Kayley use locations found on Google Street View as a starting point for stories. (Ask 'What Else Can I Do With This?', page 58.)

Sometimes, when I'm sitting inside, I think about a life of crime.

How would it have been? What would I have learnt?

Important life skills, maybe. A classical education.

I might have kept a bird, taught it to fly.

Kept it out of trouble.

Given it a break.

Project

Try telling a story using images only.
Play with two or more participants.

Divide a whiteboard, blackboard or piece of paper into six or eight equal rectangles.

One player draws a starting image in the first square. It should be what actress Ava Gardner described as 'sucker bait' – an exciting and irresistible beginning.

The other players take turns to complete the story in the successive rectangles.

Each player should aim to ensure that each successive image twists and turns the story, wrong-footing viewers by making unexpected departures. The object is to make an audience think or smile and be unable to see the ending coming.

Project

Invent and tell stories based on six random colour pictures torn from glossy magazines.

This is played with two or more participants.

Select six full-page images – use images without text and from a range of subjects, such as travel, fashion, sport, wildlife, portraiture and news.

Pin the pictures to the wall in a horizontal row, in any order.

Make up and tell short stories based on things suggested by the images and their sequence.

Use the same images to tell three different stories:

1 A drama
2 A love story
3 A ghost story

Appreciate accidents

Numerous breakthrough and innovative ideas have been as the result of accidents – including the discoveries of electromagnetic waves by Heinrich Wilhelm Röntgen, the antibiotic penicillin by Alexander Fleming, synthetic dyes by William Perkin, celluloid by John Wesley Hyatt, the microwave by Percy Spencer, solarization and photograms by Man Ray, and the first successful form of permanent photography by Louis Daguerre.

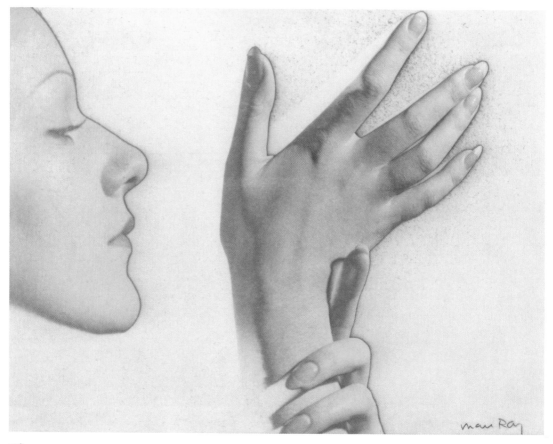

***Profile and Hands*, 1932 (opposite);**
***Untitled Rayograph*, 1922. Both Man Ray**
American-born artist Man Ray is said to
have discovered the methods to create
both solarization (opposite) and photograms
(below) following accidents in his darkroom.
Appreciating these happy accidents, rather
than throwing them away, led him to use the
techniques widely in his photographic work.

For some, these accidents solved a problem that they were seeking answers for; others, like Hyatt and Perkin, were searching for different things entirely. You have to have action in order to have an accident. All of these discoveries were made by actively pursuing ideas through experiment rather than attempting to solve problems solely in the mind. Additionally, each of these inventors was open-minded enough to know that not all accidents should be viewed as misfortunes or disasters. They understood that the results of an unexpected happening can sometimes be built upon.

Happy accidents

Be open to accident. Painters often find new forms in accidental brushstrokes or splashes of colour. Accidental results often occur for photographers, too – when taking pictures, scanning, printing images or perhaps dealing with malfunctioning equipment; these can all reveal previously unthought-of processes or techniques that can form the basis for further development. In film-making, director Nicolas Roeg recommends that you 'let the accidents happen!' (See Be Playful, page 10.)

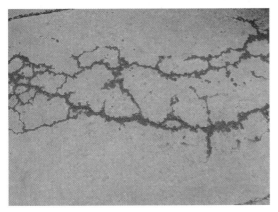

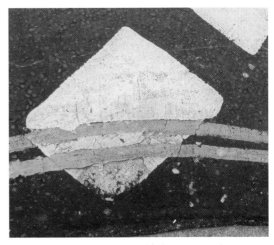

'Suddenly the lines that I'd drawn suggested something totally different, and out of this suggestion arose this picture. I had no intention to do this picture; I never thought of it in that way. It was like one continuous accident mounting on top of another.'

Francis Bacon, painter

Accidental artworks
These abstract images have been haphazardly created by happy accidents in nature, and by accidental intervention by people.

Project

Find and photograph accidental drawings – images made by the action of car tyres, footprints or cracks in roads, pavements, walls and buildings.

Talk your way in

Many areas of creativity seem to be closed shops – areas of activity that are restricted to a small group of participants. However, breaking into these arenas with a mind unburdened by the accepted and ingrained ways of doing things can lead to great innovation. Lack of entrenchment in a subject can lead to totally new ideas, perspectives and developments.

Hungarian-born designer Tibor Kalman talked his way into various fields in which his design group had little or no previous experience – for example, urban development, directing videos, real estate branding and record sleeves. Then, as design writer Peter Hall described, 'blissfully ignorant [...] the studio would try to do something that hadn't been tried before [...] this led to some astonishing successes.'

Not knowing what is thought to be impossible allows new thinking and ideas to surface, and territory to be challenged. As the physiologist Nancy Rothwell notes: 'Approach the field without necessarily enough knowledge to be drenched in what is accepted [...] you come in with a completely new view of things; what is accepted by the field can look very odd when you come in as somebody quite naïve.'

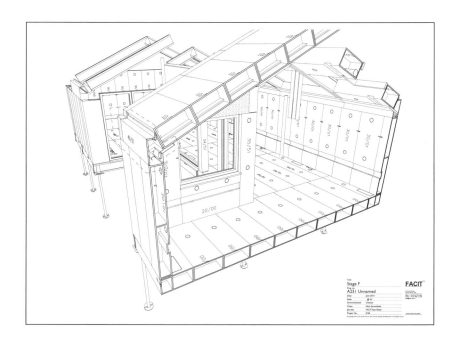

An innovative Facit Home (above)
Unburdened by any knowledge of house-building methods, and with a background in fine art and design, Bruce Bell was able to bring a completely new approach to architecture. Bell's company, Facit Homes, designs a house using a 3D computer model containing every aspect of its construction. Next, an onsite mobile factory transforms the 3D digital designs into light and easily assembled components. Then it's just like building a house from big bits of Lego. See Act Like a Kid, page 34, and www.facit-homes.com

Tom Dixon, Adidas sportswear (opposite)
Dixon's background in industrial design brought fresh thinking to his sportswear designs, including this adaptable coat, which doubles as a sleeping bag.

Project

Industrial designer Tom Dixon brings new thinking to sportswear, explaining: 'I'm not a big sportsman so I can come to the sports world with a very different attitude [...] I've always liked to be an amateur, someone who is inexperienced, and to design from a naïve perspective.'

Bring your inexperienced perspective and naïvety to an area of which you are blissfully ignorant. Choose from the following: shoe design, fashion photography, millinery, ceramics, typography or landscape architecture. You never know – your ideas may just get you in the door.

Criss-cross borders

Ideas often surface from the process of transporting thinking and inspiration across the boundaries of disciplines. However, the creative domains – art, design, science, music, film-making, dance, fashion, writing, architecture, engineering, acting, advertising, cookery and so on – are usually taught and practised in isolation.

Other creative sectors such as business, sport, politics and warfare could also be added to this list. When discoveries, strategies and practice freely move back and forth across the borders of these disciplines, exciting and innovative breakthroughs can occur. A great example is the collaboration between the fashion designer Helen Storey and chemist Tony Ryan, who shared knowledge from their own very different worlds to create Catalytic Clothing – dresses that dissolve into a form that can be easily recycled, and garments that, when exposed to light, break down pollutants in the air.

'Science is not done by sitting around thinking about things in the laboratory, it's done by talking with many different people with ideas coming in from all different kinds of areas.'

Carol W. Greider, Nobel Prize-winning scientist

Jean-Charles de Castelbajac, Andy Warhol dress, 2009
This Moroccan-born fashion designer frequently criss-crosses borders, taking inspiration from cinema, cartoons, toys, the Muppets and, here, from art.

Criss-crossing between chemistry and fashion
This giant fabric installation, created by HWKN, features the innovative catalytic cloth developed by fashion designer Helen Storey and chemist Tony Ryan.

Criss-crossing between science, cookery and design

Designers Rodrigo Garcia Gonzalez, Pierre Paslier and Guillaume Couche create the ooho – an amazing edible water bottle that could replace traditional water bottles. Drinking water is contained in a membrane made from natural ingredients. The idea crossed from seeing chef Ferran Adrià contain tasty liquids within edible spheres at his restaurant El Builli. Adria had in turn been inspired by scientific work on such membranes.

Some great developments have also surfaced in cookery, as cooks have embraced scientific knowledge, led by the pioneering Catalan chef Ferran Adrià. Leonardo da Vinci once crossed into cookery, too. When asked by a client to create a banquet he decided to automate the kitchen, designing conveyor belts to convey plates, and installing a sprinkler system in case of fire. Finding the usual staff unable to create the dishes he'd planned as miniature works of art, he employed artist friends to help out. All ended in distaster when the conveyor system broke, a fire started and the sprinklers washed away all the food. (*See also* Fail Towards Success, page 88.) And an institution that actively set out to cross borders was Bell Labs (*see also* Change the Room, page 102). They regularly invited leading young artists, composers, performers and musicians to work with their scientists, mathematicians and engineers, resulting in new developments in music, film, animation and computer graphics.

'Open yourself up to other things that can inspire you rather than looking at design constantly. You have to expose yourself to other worlds to keep your mind more active.'

Hussein Chalayan, fashion designer

Project

Criss-cross borders by working with a partner from a totally different discipline. Share knowledge and practices.

Take things literally

We are so used to using words and phrases in familiar ways that we overlook many that can gift us ideas.

For example, you could make a bulldog out of bulldog clips, a chicken out of chicken wire, make a hand rail or an armchair, knit a tank top with tanks on, or paint picture postcard and chocolate box pictures. Designer Daniel Eatock once made a passport photo of a passport, whilst the artist Dick Jewell has taken mugshots of mugs (see pages 170–71).

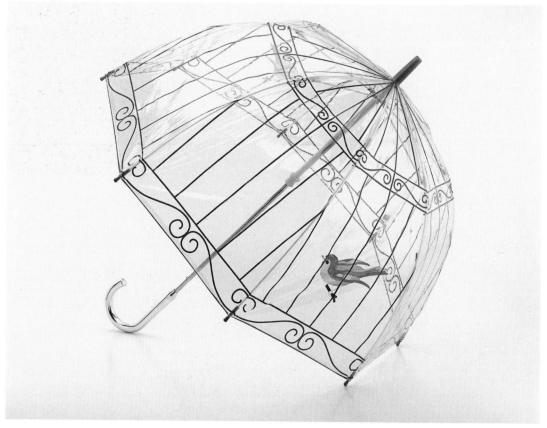

Lulu Guinness, Birdcage umbrella (opposite)
Discovering that the structure of this style of umbrella is known by manufacturers as a birdcage led iconic handbag designer Lulu Guinness to the idea for this bestselling design.

Taking things literally (this page)
Daniel Eatock's stamp stamp, a handlebar moustache, teaching guru John Brewer's coffee table book, and a pencil moustache.

Capital ideas
Design students do their
letterhead project.

Dick Jewell, *Portrait of a Nation*
(over the page)
'Mugshots' – hundreds of the mugs
offered for sale on eBay on a single day.

Project

Create a series of photos or a sculpture
inspired by taking words or phrases literally.
Look at idioms – words or phrases that,
when encountered in speech, on the page
or on screen, mean something other than
their literal sense.

Be contrary

Certain approaches and attitudes to the world are particularly conducive to the process of finding new ideas. These include enthusiasm, openness, good humour, tenacity and independence – all very positive traits. Equally important are the seemingly opposing attributes of bloody-mindedness and contrariness. These get results too.

Be contrary and stubborn in the face of things that seem certain and irreversible. Always consider the opposite. Turn things upside down in your mind. Can rust be a creative process rather than a destructive one? Can 'red-eye' improve a portrait photograph rather than be seen as a flaw? Can a video game be about building things rather than about destruction? Can drink stains improve the surface of a table? Can travelling slowly be better than travelling faster? Can music be silent? The composer John Cage boldly thought so when he composed 4'33" – 4 minutes and 33 seconds in which musicians are present but do not play their instruments. You can see performances on YouTube, and even download an app from Cage's own website.

'What I love about art students is that as soon as everyone in the industry began doing typography on computers they started carving letters out of stone.'
Sandro Sodano, designer and photographer

Contrary, opposite and reverse thinking

–Advertise your hotel by telling everyone it's terrible (see the famous campaign for the Hans Brinker Hotel in Amsterdam).
–Put your hand up if you don't have a question.
–A lost owner poster.
–'I was too well to attend.'
–A matchbox made entirely out of bits of the Taj Mahal.
–Where did it all go right?

Writer Evelyn Waugh once lived a day in reverse, beginning the day with brandy and cigars and ending it with breakfast.

Project

How could a movie be improved if everyone turned their phone on in the cinema? How could a performance be improved if every audience and cast member turned their phones on as the curtain rose?

Make it personal

Use things from your own life and experience to spark ideas – things that you know about yourself or your family, and things from your background.

As Al Jean, one of the original writers of *The Simpsons*, says, 'you get ideas from real life. Teachers you had, problems your kids are going through, things that happened to you as a kid, things you read in the paper.'

'If you are aware of something about yourself which you think is not a particularly attractive trait of your personality, rather than trying to correct it you throw it into the creative process so nothing is bad, all your dysfunctions and deficiencies can be fertilizer for the character.'

Steve Coogan, writer and actor, creator of numerous comic characters

'For a photo to be great, the photographer himself has to be part of the picture. I mean by this that the more of himself, his views, his prejudices, his nostalgia shows through, and the more the photographer is committed, the more the picture will have a chance of being unique and beautiful.'

Henry Wolf, graphic designer and writer

Project

Rewrite your own history by creating a scene from *The Simpsons* based on your own experiences.

Understand your process

To have ideas quickly and repeatedly it's vital to understand which conditions make you personally most creatively productive. Russian composer Tchaikovsky reflected: 'If we wait for the mood, without endeavouring to meet it halfway, we easily become indolent and apathetic.'

On the lash
In order to create this painting *Snow Storm – Steam-Boat off a Harbour's Mouth*, the artist J. M. W. Turner is said to have had himself lashed to the mast of a steamship in order to fully experience a storm at sea.

Pick your tools
The conditions that make us most
creative are unique; understand the
arrangement of things that fit you best.

Reflect on your successes with the different suggestions outlined in this book. Which activities, environments and collaborations put you in the most conducive state of mind for having great ideas? Spot which routines, times of day, break times and sleep times work best to promote your conscious and unconscious thinking.

Project

Discover the creative process of your ideas heroines and heroes. Some are wonderfully eccentric:

German poet Friedrich Schiller found he worked best to the smell of rotting apples.

Painter J. M. W. Turner had himself tied to the mast of a steamship so that he could paint storms.

French novelist Marcel Proust preferred to write in bed, in a cork-lined room that completely banished sound.

Winston Churchill and French novelist Colette also both wrote in bed – although not together ...

American comedian Jerry Seinfeld only ever writes on yellow pads of paper.

Just in time

Just as your mind is spinning when first encountering a challenge – see Value First Ideas, page 26 – it is also in an accelerated state as a deadline looms. The word 'deadline' comes from a line around the edge of a prison camp that, if crossed by a prisoner, would result in that prisoner being shot!

This pressure, coupled with all the earlier experience gained in the process of trying to solve the problem, can often cause one final idea to gel at the eleventh hour – or even the very last minute. Though the visuals or prototype may be complete and the presentation rehearsed, never ignore this final idea, as it may be your best.

In commercial creativity some practitioners deliberately choose to pace their creative process so that this pressured intensity is a key element in completing projects – just in time. (*See also* Understand Your Process, page 176, and Fence Yourself In, page 143.)

Ticking clocks
As a deadline apporaches, we enter a different state of mind.

Project

....

Experiment with leaving it until the last minute. Collect and collate your deadline ideas. Think of a title for this collection.

Practise,
practise, practise

The more you practise solving problems and finding ideas that work, the easier it gets. You will develop a greater understanding of the methods, processes, activities and types of thinking that produce results for you, and become more confident in your own abilities.

Hopefully this book has provided you with some new ideas-seeking habits that will lead you to a mother lode of good ideas.

THAT'S ALL FOLKS!!

Tourist: 'How do you get to Carnegie Hall?' New Yorker: 'Practise, practise, practise!'

Famous joke

'It's a funny thing, the more I practise, the luckier I get',

Gary Player, champion golfer

Practice makes perfect
Practise having ideas and getting things inside your head into those of others.

Index

Picture Credits

The author and publisher would like to thank the following institutions and individuals who provided images for use in this book. In all cases, every effort has been made to credit the copyright holders, but should there be any omissions or errors the publisher would be pleased to insert the appropriate acknowledgement in subsequent editions of this book.

Author's images:
8, 9, 11, 13, 14, 15TL, 15R, 33, 36TL, 36TR, 38, 40, 41, 42, 43, 45, 47, 48, 49, 54, 55, 60, 61, 62, 63, 68, 69, 72, 73, 85, 86, 87, 89, 94, 97T, 103, 104, 105, 107, 112, 113, 114, 115, 116, 118, 119, 121, 122, 123, 126, 127, 128, 129, 135, 141, 143, 145, 147, 150, 151, 155, 158, 159, 165, 167TR, 167B, 168,169, 174, 177, 179

10 Frederick Wilfred, Two Boys Fighting with Sticks, no date. © Museum of London

12 Otto Umbehr, Joseph Albers and students. c 1928. © Phyllis Umbehr/ Galerie Kicken Berlin/DACS 2015

15BL Picture courtesy Hans Brinker Budget Hotel, Amsterdam

16 Courtesy Tom Mitchell

17 Design by: Brian Buirge + Jason Bacher, Image Provided Courtesy of Good Fucking Design Advice

18 Johnny Firewater

19L Laura Martin

19R BA Graphic Design archive, University of Gloucestershire

20 Rod Shaw

23 Courtesy Danese, Milan

25 Courtesy Jimmy Turrell

26 Paul Bradbury/Getty Images

28 Courtesy Moritz Waldemeyer

29 Courtesy Catwalking

30 Image courtesy Mary Katrantzou

31 Moving Platforms by PriestmanGoode. www.priestmangoode.com

32 Images courtesy of Seymour Powell

35 Private collection, London

36BL Courtesy Cut Magazine

36BR © WENN UK/Alamy

37 © Benoit Tessier/Reuters/Corbis

39 Peter Dench/Reportage/Getty Images

42CR Sheep Chair, 2011, Dominic Wilcox

44 ©British Motor Industry Heritage Trust

46T ©Victoria and Albert Museum, London

46B Jack Wimperis

51 Peter Kent

52 Courtesy of Pete Frame/Family of Rock Ltd.

56-57 Jonathan Garnett

58 Dan Knight, Heavenly Chorus (the inflatable bottle organ)

59 Victor Boyko/Getty Images Entertainment

64 Bottoms Up doorbell for Droog by Peter van der Jagt. Photo: Gerard van Hees. www.droog.com Droog

65 Courtesy Jack Schulze

66, 67 Private collection, London

70 Jack Wimperis

71 Courtesy Publicis/photo by Achim Lippoth

75 ©Victoria and Albert Museum, London

76-77 Courtesy the artist and White Cube

78 Mondadori Portfolio/Getty Images

79 Daniel Eatock

81 Nick Pride

82 Agency: DDB Copenhagen, Creatives: Mikkel Møller & Tim Ustrup Madsen. Photographers: Mikkel Møller & Tim Ustrup Madsen

Acknowledgements

Hats off to Jo Lightfoot, Sarah Batten and Laurence King, who helped to shape this book, Gaynor Sermon who edited it, Peter Kent for his excellence in helping to gather the pictures and Charlie Smith for the design.

Thanks to students in Shanghai, Suzhou, Dalian, London and Gloucestershire for trying out the projects.

Many thanks are also due to the following people for their invaluable contribution to this book: Chris J Bailey, Dan Knight, Nina Saunders, Stan Wilson-Copp, Rod Shaw, Jack Schulze, Dominic Wilcox, David Myerson, Christine Bailey, Jerome Bailey, Elizabeth Bailey, Jack Southern, Mark Unsworth, Nick Pride, Jen Whiskerd, Stuart Wilding, Tim Adams, Trudie Ballantyne, Sharon Harper, Kieren Phelps, Piers Wall, Ruth Edge, Johnnie Shand Kydd, Jack Wimperis, Paul Grellier, Harley Grellier, Sarah Jackson, Paul Jackson, James Kriszyk, Jonathan Garnett, Chi Kwan, Tom Mitchell, Leah Duery, Heather Gromley, Charlotte Brooks, Lucy Blowing, Charlie Beeson, Nicola Summerville, Lisa Lavery, Jenny Yevgeniya Kuznetsova, Sirius Choi, Farida Sobhi, Bright Matithep Subsakul , Dan Glaister, Ali Glaister, Bashy Glaister, Stanley Glaister, Nathan Glaister Garcia, Maddy Guinness, James Moores, Dan Chadwick, David Fitzsimons, James Reed, Taba Reed, Patrick Reed, Aidan Reed, Harry Reed, Tessa Reed, Rosie Reed, Ben Hough, Pavlos Kyriacou, Jimmy Turrell, Dick Jewell, Cléon Daniel, Louis Jones, Amanda Jones, Jo Leahy, Neil Walker, Aya Abou-Taha, Gela Jenssen, Jenny Robinson, Jingyang Lin, Jackie Yang Fan, Johnny Firewater and Dusty Baxter-Wright.

Thanks also to the following supporters, collaborators, consigliere and inspirations: John Brewer, Nigel Langford, Kevin Jones – CFC and bar, Blaise Douglas, Kate Vincent-Smith and Red Saunders.

Dedicaton:
For Mo, Sarah and Umar.
p g a t p